SPIRITUAL NUGGETS

MARY TRIPPLEHORN SPENCER

SPIRITUAL NUGGETS

MARY TRIPPLEHORN SPENCER

Copyright © 2018 by Mary Tripplehorn Spencer

All rights reserved. This book or any portion thereof may not be reproduced or used in any manner whatsoever without the express written permission of the publisher except for the use of brief quotations in a book review or scholarly journal.

First Printing: 2018

Book Formatting & Cover Designs by Tamzin Tilley

ISBN: 978-0-359-27549-6

Ordering Information
Please Contact: Mary Tripplehorn Spencer
mtkspencer@gmail.com

TABLE OF CONTENTS

PART ONE
The Truth of the Kingdom of God...1
Praise...8
Repentance...12
Advantage of Kingdom Living..17
Spiritual Levels...19
Pride..27
God's Plan...31
Forgiveness..36
The Cleansing Process..41
Body, Soul, and Spirit...45
God's Gentle Conviction..49
Cultivating Good Habits..52
Formula for Sin..55
Effective Christian..59
Becoming an Overcomer..61
Divorce..64
New Beginnings...67
Faith..70
Chance...72
Forgiveness Again..75
Spiritual Growth...79
Warning..86

PART TWO
God's Chosen...91
The Chosen Few...93
A Denarius A Day..100
The Standard Bearer...103
The Love of Jesus...108
The Pain of Life's Challenges...110
Bottom Line...112
Fasting...113
The Transfer to God's Kingdom...119
Which Bible Should I Use..123
Where Should I Start Reading the Bible..126
What's The Deal With Satan..128

If There Is Only One God Why Are There So Many Churches........139
How Can I Know What Church To Attend......................................143
The Baptism of the Holy Spirit..148
What About TV Evangelists...160
Is The Devil Real..165
The Reality of Religion..166
The Silent Witness...173
My Faithful Father..176
In Closing..181

FORWARD

This is a series of teachings for those who are hungry for God. There is no specific order, as spiritual growth is not a step by step process, as is learning to read or mathematics. I hope you will let the Holy Spirit speak to you, and you will contemplate each truth as I share these nuggets of knowledge I learned along the way.

PART ONE

THE TRUTH OF THE KINGDOM OF GOD

I come to realize as I was being taught through the years, there was one lesson no one seemed to teach, and that is the truth of the Kingdom of God.

I knew Satan had entered the Garden of Eden and taken the headship of the kingdom from Adam. If I wanted to substantiate that truth I could read in the book of Matthew, where Jesus was baptized. Jesus came up from the water, then went into the desert to pray and fast. He was there forty days. While there Satan came and tempted him with several different things, one was about the Kingdoms; 'Look at all these Kingdoms Satan said to Jesus, I will give them all to you if you will bow down and worship me." Jesus answered, "no way Hosea." Whose Kingdoms were they? Satan's! So Satan is in control of the kingdom of this world we live in!

Now lets get on the same page. What is a kingdom? Webster's says it is a land ruled by a King. So it's not the planets, or the order of the world, the climates or weather patterns, but localities, such as the United States. So in other worlds, the nation we live in is ruled by Satan. It could be said he has the right to "woo" you anyway he wants, and his goal is to lead you into bondage that will keep you from God, a productive life, and eternal hell. Let us remember the kingdom we live in is ruled by a King, it is not a democracy.

Now let us look at Satan's kingdom. It consists of trees, and flowers, animals of all kinds, water, grass, food, crops, people, you name it, and in each of these products you will see an ever changing drama. A flower grows from a tiny seed and becomes a colorful floral design, and then dies. A tree grows and spreads it's branches, radiates a luster of life and then dies. A human being starts as an infant, grows to become an adult, reaches it's peak and then dies. In the spirit of the human race, man makes every effort to become what they can be, reach the top and then fights to keep it because someone is after it. So there is a continuous cycle in this kingdom to work your way to the top and fight to keep it, all things have a cycle, even iron rusts. So there is a cycle to everything in this kingdom, but in the end we will be reduced to nothing, for the finality of everything is death and decay and that is the final promise of this world, in Satan's kingdom.

But there is another Kingdom, the Kingdom of God. The elements of this kingdom are different. All things work for good, the cycle does not work downward, instead it is just the opposite. Everything is free from this negative drawing power. If you take a leprous arm and put it in the kingdom of God it would be healed. Healing is not a miracle in the Kingdom of God, it is the ultimate make-up of the kingdom. Working together for good, increasing, growing, improving, becoming whole, drawing near to God becoming Christ-like. Study the scriptures, see how God challenges us to reject the natural way of life in this world and put on Christ. Learn to practice love, why, because in the kingdom of God, love abides, as we practice God's way, all things become whole and perfected through love. Now if all this is true, what are you trying to tell me. I'm glad you asked!

Realize that once you have accepted Jesus Christ as your savior---and committed your life to Him, then your not under the kingdom of this world's power, your in the kingdom of Heaven. New rules, new power, new help, new hope, new protection, new promises. It is a spiritual kingdom. We must learn to adapt to the kingdom of God by using His principles, as we do, we become slowly transformed into His kingdom. Scripture says it best, Romans 12:1, do not be conformed to this world, but be ye transformed by the renewing of your mind. In other words as we read God's Word it enlightens our understanding and we become transformed little by little, we have a part to play.

Look at it this way: You have just married a person from England and you are going to live there. "Oh" new rules, new driving rules, new tax rules, new government rules, new-new-new. Your going to live there, so you adapt to their rules, if you go to England you drive on the other side of the road....well you better adapt and make the changes if your going to live there and benefit by their system. It doesn't matter where you go there is change it doesn't matter if it seems right or wrong to you it is their system. In order to benefit from their principles you need to adapt to their way. Eventually you get so used to their system it becomes a part of you. If you were going to live in the kingdom of God and benefit from the promises God has made, we need to adapt to His way of loing things.

Now here is the problem. We get saved and have the peace of knowing we are going to heaven when we die. Some may grow and adapt to some of the rules of the kingdom of God, don't lie, don't cheat or steal etc. Most certainly believe God will answer our prayers. However we continue to live by the rules of the kingdom of this world, in other words, if we are cheated, we are going to get even, if someone hits us we will hit them back, if we experience a great injustice we are not about to forgive. We may feel the right to sue someone, even though we are conscious of lying, stealing and a few other things, we still walking this world's way. We may believe in some of the concepts of the kingdom of God, such as healing or an occasional miracle, but for the most part we do not expect anything of spiritual greatness. Many times we think it has to do with a persons worthiness. We have not understood we have been removed for Satan's kingdom and are now under God's kingdom. There's no measuring line. We have a new King, a new headship, and everything in this new kingdom works for good, to my advantage and to my health and happiness.

We have been transported into the kingdom of God-we have moved--to where we have new rules, new privileges, but! we still seem to be unable to expect new hopes and new expectations because our faith is based on old world standards. If we want and expect to have the privileges of the kingdom of God's promises we must adapt to His way of doing things. We are not under Satan's rule any more, we have a new ruler who wants to protect, provide, and move us into a new realm of lifestyle. If you moved to England and want to keep doing your own things, such as drive on the opposite side of the road---hang on, there's going to be a problem very soon, When we don't adapt...it creates a problem, and we loose the benefits.

Yes, Jesus says to obey the law of the land, I can only drive 65 miles an hour in a 65 mile zone and so on. But there are many things in the kingdom of God we need to get hold of so we can lead a victorious life.

Lets take this scripture and apply it. "I can do all things through Christ." What does that mean? In this worlds kingdom if I have a problem it will only get taken care of in relation to my abilities, talents or connection.

In the kingdom of God, with the same problem, I have access to God's power, wisdom, knowledge, understanding and discernment. The answer is not dependent on me, but my faith in God and I can reach outside of my worlds understanding and expect supernatural help. I can expect God to intervene. I can expect God to make a way where there is no way. When I am presented with situations beyond my capabilities, I am dependent on God, and I can do all things through Christ. I've just raised the bar on my ability to do things, I'm not dependent on my attributes any more. I'm dependent on my faith through Christ.

If you get a little "Bible Promise Book," and study the promises, understand they are yours. Work on making an image of the Kingdom of God, it's rules and regulations. Recognize your living in a new world, and not subject to the kingdom of this world, Let me tell you one terrific advantage of this kind of understanding.

When we live in this world and need a favor from God such as a healing, a new job, a financial breakthrough, we are only as good as how we feel. If I'm spiritually up then I can boldly proclaim it. But if I'm down... my response is: I'm not good enough, I've just blown it, God can't help me now, I don't deserve it. All these value's are dependent on how I measure up with what I think I should be. That is not spirituality. That's this world's thinking. God didn't ask you for anything. "You have to be good enough!" No, you don't have to reach a level five before you can ask for that. No...no...no...all that is this world's thinking.

Look at it this way, when you moved to England there was a law that said every time you pass this light you get ten points, eventually you have a hundred points. Now you get a ticket but you can take your hundred points and apply it towards your ticket and be free. Did that law have anything to do with your goodness or badness? No...you just worked the system. The same thing happens when you move to the kingdom of God, different rules, not based on your qualifications or abilities. In this world we measure how good, how smart, how pretty or handsome we are, everything has a measuring line, but not the kingdom of God. If you learn the system of God's kingdom you can override a lot of pitfalls, and a lot of setbacks. It is up to me to activate the principles of the kingdom of God. Jesus is our measuring line.

PRAISE

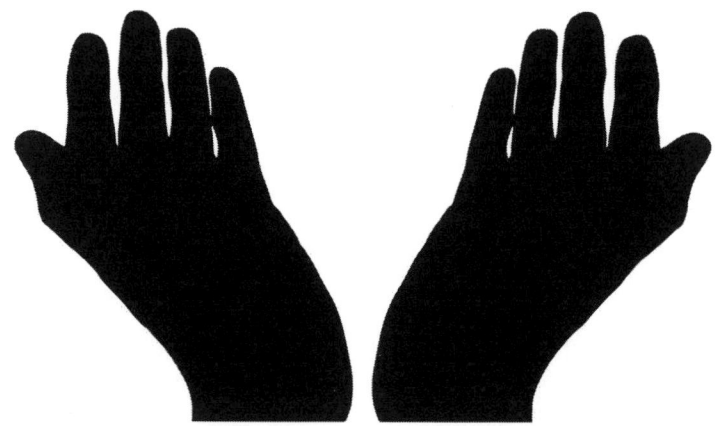

When we think of growing in the ways of God, we often think it will be like math or reading, I must learn 1+1=2; 2+2=4 and so on. Step by step but, the process of spiritual growth does not come in a systematic way. It seems to pick up right where your at, and when you need it the most, as you seek it.

I read a book on praise, in which the author commented, how the sacrifice of praise breaks the hold over whatever trial you are experiencing. It is right at hand and doesn't need to wait until your on level four. Now I must be honest, you may need to be on level four before you can walk on water! But don't confuse level four in the spiritual with grade four in school.

Have you noticed in your early walk with God, how thankful you were, and how you gave God the glory for an array of the littlest good things you experienced.

Previously we didn't really see it. Then all of the sudden we see the beauty of a flower! It was always there, but now our eyes have been opened to new things and we are aware of how God is intertwined in our daily life. We realize some of the good things that happened to us are not necessarily just a break, but that God has interceded on our behalf and blessed us. It becomes quite commonplace to praise God for all the littlest things that happen to us. As we grow spiritually, we read how scripture calls us to praise God in **all things**, however it generally doesn't really sink in for quite some time, I mean to praise God when something bad happens seems a bit sacrilegious. We often sing the song "We bring the sacrifice of Praise", but they are just words to a song, until comes the time when there will be a need for a sacrifice of praise.

One day we hit a wall, the joy of the Lord is gone and we cry buckets of tears. We frantically search for a way out of whatever predicament we've gotten into, but nothing helps. Then we remember those words, praise God in all things, praise God in the midst of the storm."Yes Praise."

One of my experience's to praise God in the midst of a storm was when my husband and I had just closed our seasonal business. I picked up the little metal cash box which had all the money we had saved up to help us through the winter months.

I put the box on the floor of my car and stopped by the coffee shop to tell my husband something. I ran in and right out, but in that fraction of time, someone had taken a hammer from my husband's truck and broke the window in my car and took the box and ran. After talking to the police I went right back to our business and began to walk back and forth in the parking lot, with tears running down my cheeks, I praised God. My teeth were clenched and my heart sank, but I kept praising God for at least an hour.

The next morning as I went by the place it happened, I saw a police car out by the river. I stopped, and as I came up to them, they were going through the contents that had been in my little metal box. The box had been thrown into the river, but most of the money and much of the contents were there on the ground. You can be sure I gave God the glory. I've had many opportunities to praise God in the midst of a storm, and God has worked mightily every time. I really believed the man dropped the box contents and threw the box into the river the minute I started to praise. Praise loosed the power of God to intercede.

One would ask, what is the key or how does it work. Is God just doing a miracle, or is there some principle that praise invokes. We must always keep in mind we are dealing with the spiritual. But know that all spiritual action is proceeded by the Word of God. Remember in the Kingdom of God, all things work for good. Know also that the Word is light and light penetrates the darkness. Also the Word is the sword of the Spirit. So when we praise, we are obeying the Word, penetrating the darkness to release the light into the darkness. It is the spirit of God overcoming the power of Satan. It is vital for a spiritual walk to understand that the key to victory, is applying the word of God. What I have often experienced is when I praise, God opens my eyes to the real problem. He often gives me wisdom or understanding, I then recognize how to deal with the situation, or it just devolves with understanding. But it is always a supernatural exchange or experience. So realize praise works as a spiritual weapon against the enemy, and there can be victory. The sacrifice of Praise is probably the easiest and most effective principle God has made available.

REPENTANCE

The first year of my new Spirit-filled life was the most wonderful year of my life. I read stories of other peoples experience, even in history, yet saw no experience any greater then my own. God literally did miracles through me. But by the end of the year, it was though God had disappeared. Day after day I prayed and yet there was no response. I felt as though He had literally abandoned me.

One day I was in the City of Owosso, and as I walked by a book store, I decided to go in. I can still see myself and my terrible dejected spirit. I found a book by some Christian woman of influence and began to read it. In the book she talked about going to her first prayer meeting, and how they recommended she seriously examine her conscience and take care of any old business. As she did this, she came up with three things she felt she needed to deal with. I think she had cheated on a test when she was in high school, I don't remember the other two things.

She ended up writing a letter of apology to her teacher and then took care of the other two things. But she made each one right by confessing her sin to them.

So I thought, well maybe that's what I need to do. So I began to do some soul searching, and it didn't take long to to find I had a few things that needed to be dealt with as well. I think I felt like I needed to come up with at least three things like the lady did, and of course it was easy as I examined my conscience. I sent a letter to each person and explained that I had given my life to Christ and was reminded of my sin. I remember, that as I dropped those letters into the mailbox, God came back full force.

Now this was a new development, I had confessed what I thought was all my sins when I got Spirit Filled. As I pondered this experience I remember the scripture saying we are to be changed into His likeness. I realized that God's not done with me yet, and that He will continually reveal areas in my life to cleanse and purify so that I may become a vessel for Him to dwell in. More of thee and less of me.

Now let me share one more thing on this subject. Twenty five years later I was taking care of an old man who had Alzheimer's. His wife had died the year before. He lived in the country in a modest little house and all he did was sit and watch television. I fed him his meals, but the house was already spotless and I had nothing to do.

One day I decided to take my mending along to help fill in the time. I took my small sewing kit and got out a needle. As I tried to thread the needle the eye was too small for me to see. I thought, well this guys wife must have had a sewing kit and maybe she will have a larger needle. However, when I found her sewing basket, I discovered she had a needle threader in it. Now a needle threader is a tiny object that comes free when you buy needles. It enables you to thread any needle regardless of size. When I finished my mending I was about to put back the needle threader in her basket, when it came to me. This old lady is dead now, and this poor old soul is never going to use it, but it is something I know I can use, so I kept it.

Now big deal, it's a free object when you buy needles, and when this guy dies, it will go to the auction block in a big box with a dozen other seemingly useless items. Sometime later, maybe months, maybe years, I don't remember, but I was having hard time communicating with God. I started fasting and praying again and making every effort to get through to God, but to no avail. Then one day as I was praying I would see this little image of a needle threader, I just pushed aside the thought and went on, next day same thing happened, but it was so trivial I once again pushed the thought or and the picture aside. The third day when it came up I said "really God" you can't be serious. I got out my paper and wrote a letter to the people and told them I had taken the needle threader and was returning it. Just like that --once again --I was set free.

God is faithful and wants a pure heart, and He is so merciful to convict us even on the tiniest level. When God revealed Himself to us and we accepted Jesus as our savior, we were convicted of our sins. I am sure we all repented and then rejoiced at our salvation. But in truth we only confessed those sins we were convicted of, and at the time that seemed as though that's all God wanted. It was just obvious sins we felt compelled to confess. We didn't go deeper because we didn't know there was anything deeper, and at the moment we felt as though we had cleaned the slate.

The truth is there may be a whole back-log of sins yet to confess. In God's mercy He brings conviction only as He sees fit, maybe just what we can handle at the time. We must understand it is a lifelong process.

This is not a popular point of view, but I am convinced, that if we have come to a standstill in our spiritual walk, or feel God has abandoned you, then you might consider doing some soul searching. One more very unpopular point of view is this, though God may want us to repent to Him, there may also be times when He wants you to make it right with the one we've offended.

Realize there are times when God may be digging up a territory that you have practically forgotten, or He may be turning over some recent missed offense. Regardless, if He didn't love you so much He would leave you in the darkness, but because He want you to transformed into His likeness He will continue to visit you as needed.

ADVANTAGE OF KINGDOM LIVING

Lets look at this picture, you own a small business and need to make payroll for several people each week. But the end of the month your finances are exhausted, but you still have to make payroll. In this world, you can borrow enough money to cover, but that only puts you in deeper. The next week you will have twice the amount needed. You've already knocked on all the doors of those who still owe you money to no avail. Bottom line, no paychecks, which leave you disgruntled employees, bad reputation and very depressed. The black cloud is hanging over your head and you carry it into every aspect of you life. "This kingdom" downward spiral. I'm responsible, I'm a failure, it was all up to me!

Now lets imagine we're in the kingdom of God. Same scenario, but wait, how can I apply kingdom living to this. First, I remind myself, I'm now in the kingdom of God, I begin to repeat scriptures; I can do all things through Christ; I am the head and not the tail; my Father owns the cattle on a thousand hills; God shall supply all my needs according to His riches. I am exactly where God put me doing exactly what he called me to do; I have been obedient to God, I have tithed, therefore it is His problem, not mine and He is more than capable of handling this situation. As I begin to repeat these scriptures out loud over and over, I begin to get giddy, I'm actually smiling now! Wow...how is God going to do this? In walks a contractor who just picked up a job and is paid his one third in advance for the job, and what do you think yes, yes, yes, he decided to pay for his cement in advance. It covers my payroll to the penny. This is a true story and has been repeated many times.

When we take ourselves out of the picture, take a little inventory, am I in order with the way I've handled my responsibilities? I'm living in the Kingdom of God and able to apply all God says in the Word. Thats what it's there for. You can take any problem and find the scripture to fix the problem, I don't need to measure myself with am I good enough, do I deserve help, bottom line...He's my Father and wants to help me. It's not about me it's about God.

SPIRITUAL LEVELS

Level One - Lobby Living

There are many stages in the spiritual life, lets break down these stages so we can begin to evaluate as to where we are.

First we realize there is a heaven, but then we learn there are some hoops we need to jump through before we get there. God reveals Himself to us and we accept Jesus Christ as our Savior, we are now at level one. I call it the lobby. If we have been fortunate enough to have had an influence of Christian thought then we recognize there are also rules in this kingdom. I will simplify this by recognizing the ten commandments as these basic rules. Now lets say we join a church, we feel good, right? We get a little involved, help with the funeral dinners, or building a porch with the men's ministries.

In lobby living we begin to work hard on the commandments, but we also begin to see the imperfection of those around us who claim to be the perfection of a Christian church member, and yet fall short hmmm.....very short. After some time I also realize I can't seem to break the hold over my own sinful habits. I miss church one Sunday, and then later another, and before long I can't remember just why I went in the first place, or I got my feeling hurt, and now I'm not going to be among those hypocrites. Well Satan won that one, you may claim to be a Christian, but you won't have a testimony or be an example of Christ. There are many lobby liver's who stay in church and make it their social base, not really open to the Word. The world is full of lobby liver's, in my estima tion probably more then half of the church members are ineffective examples of Christ-like lifestyle. As they say, talk the talk, but don't walk the walk.

Then there is level two Christian.

They get downright serious about being a Christian, and are going to make sure everyone around them is going to know it. They push, push, push. Your going to hear the gospel pushed right down your throat, they are not so serious about their own walk, once they got saved the figure they got it all, and now they spend their time pushing it on you. They run down every church around them, and if you don't accept Christ you are a heathen. They are very inclusive, they are the only ones with the truth and any idea outside of their understanding makes you surely a child of the devil.

Now we move the level three:

Level three has spent much time lobby living, but instead of giving up, they realize they don't seem to have the power to overcome their bad habits, or sinful ways. They hear of the Holy spirit. When the hunger came for the Holy Spirit, they realize not only do you accept Jesus Christ as your Savior and commit your life to Him, but you invite the Holy Spirit into your life as well. In level one you have Jesus in your heart, but your still calling the shots, your running the show, what color car to buy, who to marry, where to work, all the choices of life, there is no effort to call on God, after all He gave me a brain didn't he! But in level three you give your life to Him, you yield your desires and wants, because you come to realize God wants more for you then you can dream. He want's to help you come into alignment with His will so you can fulfill your hearts desire and walk in perfect harmony with Him, God has a plan for your life.

In lobby living there are many who realize they can't make the mark, and leave due to someone's insensitivity and decide they don't need this in their life, they often feel they have failed, because they couldn't seem to get into the spiritual level they desired. Or they see the worldliness of the body of Christ and feel they can do better than that without going to church. Lobby living is like driving a stick shift, you are in charge of every action, to gear up or gear down, and some do it better then others. The key to understanding lobby liver's is to understand that though they accepted Jesus christ into their heart as they savior, there really was no commitment to yield their life to Christ and follow Him. Therefore, in not yielding themselves to Christ they still called the shots of their lives. They make all the decisions in their life, without seeking God's direction. Their main goal is to have a nice life with all the trimmings, right schools, colleges, who to marry, what house to buy or what job they wanted, They were falsely led to believe, all they needed was to accept Christ into their lives and they were saved, and through they may change a few things in their lives they were still in the drivers seat as to decisions about directions in their life. The denominational Pastors failed to impress on them that salvation was only a beginning, God never intended the church to be run by lobby liver's. For the most part many churches are not more then denominational social clubs and their congregation just want to stick around so the church can bury them.

Now lets look at sixty percent Christians. They are denominational saints. The've been through trials, and have found peace through faith in God. Every church has a few sixty percenters. Those people who are forgiving, cover others, make peace, always have a good word, are genuinely kind loving people, only see the good in others. There goal in life was just to have a good life, they made the most of their challenges and learned to apply scriptures, so that when you listed the fruit of the spirit, love, joy, peace, patience etc, they have achieved the goal. They are no lobby-livers, they have moved to the sanctuary and taken the Word into their hearts.

Now who are one hundred percent Christian. Now that we understand lobby liver's, lets take the next step, our wonderful God who sees how pathetic the state of our spirituality is, sends revival approximately every twenty years. It's kind of a spotty thing but a true revival spreads like wildfire.

It started in the **Acts of the Apostles. Acts 1:4, and being assembled together with them, He (Jesus) commanded them not to depart from Jerusalem, but to wait for the promise of the Father, which He said, "you shall be baptized with the Holy Spirit not many days from now." You shall be witness to Me in Jerusalem and in all Judea and to the ends of the earth. Jesus told them that He must go, and when He goes He will send the Holy spirit.**

Now what happened Acts 2:1 " Now when the Day of Pentecost had fully come, they were all with one accord in one place, and suddenly **there came a sound from heaven, as of a rushing mighty wind, and it**

filled the whole house where they were sitting. Then appeared to them divided tongues as of fire and one sat upon each of them and they were all filled with the Holy Spirit and began to speak with other tongues, as the Spirit gave them utterance."

What is this! Now you say, thats just what happened in Bible days, what has that got to do with us? Lets take a look at this. Jesus never put a time table on the infilling of the Holy Spirit, and history records spiritual outbreaks for 2000 years that are accompanied by tongues of fire. When Jesus told them to build the church or spread the gospel, He told them to wait for the Holy Spirit. You can't build a church with out the guidance of the Holy spirit. The problem with lobby livers they are trying to spread the gospel with head knowledge with out the Spirits direction. There is nothing in the flesh that can do the work of the Holy Spirit. It takes Holy spirit power to walk with God and do the works of God. It takes an understanding that He is, our God, our deliver, our master. Remember a Kingdom is run by a King. We have King Jesus as our leader. He will lead you in all truth, He will deliver you out of bondage, He will build the church.

We are recognizing today that Christ not only want's us to be in Christ, but to be filled with the Holy Spirit. Do not be deceived into believing you received it at salvation, you received a portion of it, but until you yield and commit your life to Christ you have not received the fulness of the Holy Spirit. Until you are willing to obey His every word, not my will but thy will be done and understand your flesh, your brain cannot set you free. Christianity is a spiritual power that overpowers the King of this world, Satan. The flesh is under the control of Satan, and a church who thinks they can brainstorm a direction for a church can never raise above Satan's plans. Oh they my do good works, but they can only raise to the limit the flesh can expect. Now he will want you to think your doing good, because God help you if you get wind of the truth.

Following WWI the church seemed to forget about holiness, we had a moral world, why push people any deeper, but Christ calls us to holiness, to become like Him.

The true Christian is one who gets Spirit filled, and begins to walk with God. He lives in the promise "I can do all things through Christ," "nothing formed against me shall prosper," " that by the stripes of Jesus I am healed." we have a Bible full of promises for deliverance from drug addition or bondage from violent expressions, from the lies that Satan wants us to believe. We enter a world where we have an opportunity not only to spread the Word and enlarge the Kingdom, but to fulfill the potential God created us for. Jesus through the Holy Spirit sets us free. This is the spiritual life that God intended the church to have from the very beginning. Read the book and ask God to open your eyes! Your not playing church in the lobby anymore, your in the sanctuary giving glory to God.

# PRIDE

In the early years of my spiritual development, I had about twelve-to fifteen close friends who were all in the Spirit. We had weekly meeting and spent a lot of time together during the week. We spent much time discussing our spiritual growth, as well as each others. I remember a conversation about one of our friends in the group who had a lot of pride. I ended the conversation by saying, how glad I was that tho I had many challenges, pride wasn't one of them. I shudder at that remark and how foolish I was.

Interesting enough fifteen years later, I had another bout with pride. I had been seeking God with prayer and fasting. About the second day I had a vision. I saw a beautiful iceberg floating in the middle of what appeared to be the Alaska waters. It was large and alone. The rays of the sun glanced off of it and produced a multitude of colors, it was beautiful. Wow I thought, then I heard God say, "that is you." Oh my, I was humbled, so beautiful, how could that be, then He said yes, your so hard that when I try to get something through to you it just bounces off. I was crushed. Then he showed me a small dam, the water crossed under a road, and the dam was regulated by a series of boards, to control the water they either added or removed some of the boards. However, there were as many as eight boards on top of each other and the water filtered between them all. In my vision I saw the iceberg floating down the stream, but when it got to the boards in the dam it could not go any farther. God said, that I needed to become like a drop of water, because a body of water can move a mountain but an iceberg can do nothing. I don't think I lifted my head for two days, how terrible, you talk of pride. I spent the rest of my life consciously checking for pride.

Daniel 5:20 says, "Pride hardens the mind"; Psalms 10:12 says, "Pride keep you from real progress"; Psalms 10:4 says, "it hinders your coming to God: Hosea 7:9 says, 'it produces spiritual decay." Those are pretty hard word for one single sin.

As I mentioned previously I considered myself very insignificant as the middle child of five. then I married a very intelligent man who, though he may not have realized it, led me to believe I was basically dumb. Now I had gotten saved when I was five and was in the

Methodist Church faithfully. I remember the wonderful stories taught to me in SundaySchool, I memorized scripture and consumed all that was possible. Because I was saved my eyes were opened to knowledge and truth which helped to form my character.

When I was about twenty two, I decided to join the Catholic Church, I was hungry for God and thought a stricter religion would help. A few years later there was a revival movement that went through all the churches, and in the Catholic church it was big. That's when I got what we called Spirit filled. God really poured out His Spirit on me and I shared it with everyone and anyone. Then God used me to get a prayer group going. Now the friends in the group were raised Catholic so the group was basically Catholic. Now interestingly enough, this new move of God was all about the Bible and scripture, and with a Methodist background I was already very familiar with scripture, however, these young Catholics were not. Their church focused on faithfulness to mass, and moral behavior, family values and many good things, but not scripture. Ooohhh honey I had the corner on the market. It felt so good to finally be in the know. I was the one who could answer questions, I already understood so much of what was going on in the movement. It just unlocked all that I had learned in the Methodist Church and more. It was so good to be in a close lationship with God and to help others, I felt like a million bucks. No longer a quiet little mouse in the corner of the room, but a real physical force in the middle of a group of hungry Christians. Now there were many good things that came out of all those years, but at the same time, I became prideful. I didn't know it at the time, I was just finally becoming a human being that had worth. Pride sneaks in. I can't say I was faced with any major difficulties because of my pride, but I remember how there were times He would bring me down in subtle ways. I was fortunate He was so merciful with me, and it may have been because I had so many areas that needed to be worked on, God is gentle and delivers us one problem at a time.

I don't know if anyone can relate to my story, but I want you to see that anytime you feel superior to others, you are in danger of pride, it will keep you from growing in your relationship with Christ. The thing I want to point out is this. I had always been focused on growing in Christ- Bible reading- prayer and fasting. This kept me sensitive to God's correction. He broke through my sinfulness and comforted me before I became hardened. If there is no discipline in your spiritual habits, your heart can become hardened and God will not be able to get through to you.

If you feel as though you can't seem to get through to God lately, then consider a thorough re-evaluation. Scripture says, "pride goeth before a fall," it also hardens the heart. Remember it's the tiny drops of water joined together that move the mountains, not the big "I."

GOD'S PLAN

I could probably list four things that kept me in the race for spiritual maturity. But first I needed to learn one thing. God had a plan for my life. When I learned that, I was astonished. God had a plan for my life! Me the most insignificant of my family, the nobody? I always saw myself as a very invisible person in my family, the middle of five, whose brothers and sisters all seemed to know where they were going, all seemed to have a plan and the energy to make it happen. I had nothing going for me that I knew of. So when God revealed to me He had a plan, I became a different person, I had value, I had promise. It didn't matter to me that I may be a nothing in the world, because now I didn't need the world's approval. I had God's. He saw me as a person of value, thats all I needed. Now let me say this to you. God has a plan for your life! You were created to fulfill a certain purpose. Get hold of that, it will change your life.

Many year ago I was given a book that revealed God having a plan for me and it followed with the teaching of what we call the gift of the Holy Spirit. After finishing the book I set it down and spent the rest of the day seeking to be filled with the Holy spirit or I might say begging God to give me the Holy spirit, and in time he so generously answered my prayer.

Now lets think a bit, What does it mean for God to have a plan for your life? If God has a plan already in place, then all I need to do is seek Him. I don't need to try and figure out what He expects me to do. If you have committed your life to Christ you can be sure God will begin to lead you into His plan. You may not recognize it at first, but eventually you will have an experience that you think, I know I didn't plan that, it just fell in place, and little by little you begin to see God interacting in the happenings of you life. Little by little you suspect you are being molded into a new creature of worth. Just keep walking.

Now if your filled with the Spirit of God you are eager to serve Him, your hungry to get out there and do something. But to be honest, it doesn't work that way. This in-filling opens the door to such a new world, it is incomprehensible to start with. Its a little like going to Disney world, when you walk through the gates there is an array of things to do, places to go, each section of the park is alluring and you want to experience them all. All of scripture is like that park, all of the sudden you could be laying hands on the sick, giving a word of wisdom, opening understanding to a person, sharing the word with power that actually effects a persons life. People are drawn to you, you have knowledge that continues to increase, you are a wonder to many people, and you think what am I going to do with all this. All of the sudden I'm somebody worthwhile, and you anxiously wonder what your calling is, cause you know He has a plan.

To be honest with you, right now His plan for you is just to absorb all this new knowledge and power, and learn. Come to know who you are in Christ. In this process, you come to see your own shortcomings and you have to deal with them. Your in a cleansing process to make you a worthy cup bearer. You find out you have very strong opinions about people and things that are actually a stumbling block to others, and it hinder's your witness. Your convicted of being a talebearer, you even see where you occasionally tell an untruth, I don't want to say lie. God is in the process of cleaning you up to make you ready to be His servant. It seems to be a back and forth action somewhat like a tennis ball in the middle of play, you have a wonderful opportunity to be used in a situation and the next thing your hit with a reality of your own shortcomings, and the need to deal with it. You are growing and you know it, you are being used and you know it. In the course of time a door opens that puts you in some form of ministry, it's small at first, but it can become widespread, however now it doesn't matter, I'm just happy to be in tune with Him, to be faithful, I am a willing servant.

Now heres the stumbling block, we so thirst for the privilege to serve, to be on that stage being used, laying hands on the sick, passing our words of knowledge, that we think, well I really believe I'm called to have this ministry and because you are unique everybody agrees with you, so you force open the door, feeling led by the Spirit, when in truth its the flesh. Just in the past five years I have watched four people start a ministry because they thought God had laid it on their heart, and today those ministries are closed.

Your greatest ministry is right where your at. You are a light in the darkness, a hope for the discouraged, a balm of Gilead for the hopeless. Your life just as it is, is spreading the gospel. If you have become a yielded saint, then you are serving God in a most powerful way. You may think your life is mundane, but I can assure you, you are hope for someone, your an encourager, your a beam of light because you are a child of God who is submitted to His will. I can assure you if God has a specific ministry for you, He will make it known to you, and He will provide a way. The truth is many people pursue ministry, but so often fail, they find themselves back to the drawing board.

The truth is they often do considerable damage to lives as they are actually out of order, not really mature enough to fulfill the ministry God has in store for them. Now I admit I wanted ministry so bad I could cry, but God didn't open the door for me until I was in my fifties. In those twenty years He taught me vital lessons, He delivered me from sin, I went through the fire of God and he brought me to maturity so that when I did go into ministry I was accountable. I have thanked God enumerable times for letting me go through the fire before I got into ministry. Needless to say, before the door opened I was not setting on the sidelines doing nothing, I was teaching Bible classes, ministering to those in need, taking in the homeless, and many other things. I can say from the very day I got Spirit filled, I never took my eyes off God. I've gone through painful situations, but never given up. My motto was, it is not a sin to fall, it is a sin not to get up. I don't know how I had the courage when I failed over and over again, but I never gave up and God brought me through. If God has a plan for you life and He does, never quit pursuing it.

FORGIVENESS

The Lord's prayer puts up front the call to forgive one another. Forgive us our trespasses as we forgive those who trespass against us. We can come to an honest understanding of the need when we consider the sacrifice Jesus made for each one of us, by erasing all our sins with His blood. Wow, one would think it would be an easy task to forgive others considering the cross.

However, forgiveness seems to be a stumbling block for many people. I was sharing something with my sister the other day and she brought up the name of someone she held a grudge against for many years. The woman was a family member and is now dead, and I too had a problem with her many years ago. I heard myself tell my sister, but you know one day I just looked at this woman's circumstances, and thought, she is family and she deserves to be loved. I have a responsibility to reach out and love her. I had to put aside all the shortcomings I felt previously, the discrepancies that had alienated us in years past and let go. As I made this choice little by little I seemed to have more compassion for her challenges and actually began to love her. Bottom line is, I made a choice and made it possible for God to work through me. Of all the many times I have needed to forgive, I will say this situation was one of the easiest, and I so immediately saw the hand of God at work in it.

The key in this situation for me was, she was family. I have always felt a real conviction from the Word that we are obligated to care for our own family, and that was the turning point for me. But it always amazed me at how much I ended up loving her, and I knew in reality it was not me, but God.

In several places I bring up how we often look at spiritual growth as we might look at learning in school, grade by grade. I usually try to make it clear it doesn't work that way. But to be honest, just as we may fail a grade and not be able to go on, and even worse have to repeat the grade, unforgiving can create that same scenario. If we come to a place God is calling us to forgive and we fail to do so, it will bring a screeching halt to our relationship with God. It's like where is God! He was here but now I just can't even reach Him, we find ourselves in a dark place, with no way to turn.

I'm going to try and do a short version of this situation, but will probably cover it elsewhere. First, there is the obvious awareness of things that need to be forgiven when you first come to Christ, I cheated on a test, I was unfaithful to husband, I stole something. These sins stand out and we quickly are convicted and deal with them. We're now moving along with Christ and feeling good, but then we hit the wall. I've often said it was like a mountain. The mountain is normally brown and dark. When we get saved all of the sudden it has been covered with snow, all white and pretty. That's me white and pretty with God. But eventually the snow on top of the mountain begins to melt and we see a black area. That will be something God wants you to deal with. It may be sin or an attitude God want's to deal with you. You search your soul and discover something that happen some years ago and you put it under the blood. Now the mountain is all white again. This is repeated many times in life over and over again. When you are ready He is going to cleanse you on a deeper level, and it goes on. Now there are times when you think, wait a minute I've dealt with this before. What your going to find, is that the mountain's center holds the root of your problems, and, you may have repented for the obvious problem, but God wants to remove the root of the problem.

There are many sins' or bad attitudes that are deep within our soul, buried and hidden. God wan't to remove them all but He is gentle and only does it as He sees fit. Let me give you an example.

I learned early to know God is often most revealed in the quiet places. I used to just set time aside and seek God by going back in my mind to my earliest memory. I would just set quietly go back, back , until God would reveal a memory. One time I went back in my mind to the time I was four years old, my birthday being in December my mom thought I could handle kindergarten. I begin to remember the teacher would give us pictures to color and I would do my best, but it was never good enough and I never got a gold star like the other kids did. It would break my heart because I would try so hard. One day she gave us a picture to color and for some reason we could take it home. I told my mother about not getting a star and she looked at the picture and said, maybe if you color each blade of grass it will make the difference. Oh, I worked on that picture so hard, I colored each blade of grass, I was so excited to take it up to the teacher, and she said, Oh Mary this is so good.... and I would give you a gold star if you hadn't painted the blades of grass. When that memory came up I cried buckets of tears. I know it was at this point I came to the conclusion that school wasn't for me, I just didn't have it, and I do really believe I just felt like, why try you can't make the grade anyway so why try. I hated school all my childhood, and was very poor in it. I think if someone had told me I was only four years old and probably not ready for school it might have made a difference. But that was for me a very emotional setback, and God knew I needed to forgive the teacher. 'his unforgiving had far reaching effects, and to be honest, I might not be the sharpest knife in the drawer, but I am not dumb and never was. But all in all God wanted to set me free, and I am amazed how loving God is and how He continues to work with us to make us the best that we can be.

Now I want to make this clear, I didn't hold a grudge against the teacher and hate her, I actually took the brunt of it on myself, I must be dumb, I don't make the grade etc. Satan used this as a mighty weapon against me, and it effected my whole life until I was in my forties. But in essence I did need to forgive the teacher, it was a hidden grudge that I didn't know I had until God revealed it.

Some call this inner healing, which it actually was, but some think you have to be prayed over, or delivered, but you don't, there are so few who know how to do deliverance right, and they get puny results. You just need to have quiet time with God, rest in Him, ponder on the thoughts He gives to you and he will reveal what he wants. To be honest with you a small percentage of people who really have a powerful salvation experience continue to grow and it is all because they have never let go of incidences that happened to them. I can't forgive my dad for treating me this way, or I can't forgive my X for his unfaithfulness and so on. Spiritual growth is relational to forgiveness. If you don't take the time to draw near to God and let him reveal your shortcomings, you will be just another blade of grass in the lawn. Oh yea saved but....

THE CLEANSING PROCESS

Romans 14:10 Therefore you are inexcusable O man, for in whatever you judge another, you condemn yourself.

When I began to walk with the Lord, I admit I had a lot of old misguided values, and was very opinionated. I didn't believe in smoking or drinking, and certainly no drugs. The word divorce was not in my vocabulary. I was somewhat against wealthy people, somehow I suspected they probably got their wealth in some crooked way. Strangely enough I wasn't prejudiced about colored people because I had rarely seen a black person, but I had a lot of other prejudice. I realize a lot of these values were formed through the beliefs of my church. We didn't believe in drinking and so on, which was a blessing for me as I was never tempted to be involved in this behavior. But it made me critical of others who were. I remember when I went to the Catholic Church to inquire about taking a series of lessons to consider joining, I knew one of their priests smoked a cigar. If he would have opened the door when I went, I very likely would never have joined the church. I also remember many years later as a Methodist Church Pastor, I saw many of the clergy stepping out back and having a smoke. That really bothered me. I still have high expectations of people in leadership positions, but in the early years of my life my opinions were really out of control.

Somewhere along the line I began to be convicted of my sinful attitude, Matthew 7:1, Judge not, least ye be judged. But what could I do to change? I could accept that maybe some of these habits were not necessarily sinful, just bad habits or even addictions. I began to think, how can you expect a child who was raised in a household of drinking and smoking be any different then their parents. What could you expect of a child who had never heard the gospel. To be honest I spent most of my time now with new Christians who were about as judgmental as I was, and I began to be a little critical of them, not having compassion on those who were bound with habits that would more than likely lead them into trouble or shorten their life.

Now I spent most of my time reading books on spiritual development, and one day I read this story.

"A couple invited Jesus to their home for dinner. Now they gussied up the living room and maybe a few other rooms so the house would look nice for Jesus. After his arrival they had a short visit then ate their meal. After eating Jesus said, well now I would like to see the other rooms in the house! What they said! The other rooms? Yes, you invited me in, and now I would like to see where I'm going to live. They reluctantly went on the grand tour of their home, the bedroom where junk had been piled, the basement that was cluttered and the nasty garage, as well as all the other rooms that needed cleaning up."

Now this story is about us, the truth is that when we invite Jesus into our hearts, He expects to live there, and most of us know, just like the house, we have a lot of cleaning up to be done. But the good news is, He only takes one room at a time, just as you clean a house one room at a time. Today He may be dealing with me about my smoking, six months from now He may address my exaggerating. Little by little He opens the door to our soul that reveal the areas where we fall short. Now I understand that if he deals with me that way, he will also deal with everyone else the same. He is no respecter of persons. He may be dealing with you about lying and your spouse about drinking. When I realized how gentle God was in dealing with my judgmental spirit, it totally took my judgmental spirit away from others and helped me to have compassion for them. I realized God is always at work, but deals with each of us in the area He see's fit.

There are two benefits in this, I can rest, because I understand it is a work of the Holy Spirit to cleanse us and make us whole. The other thing I learned, it's not my job to point out the sins of others, it's my job to love them.

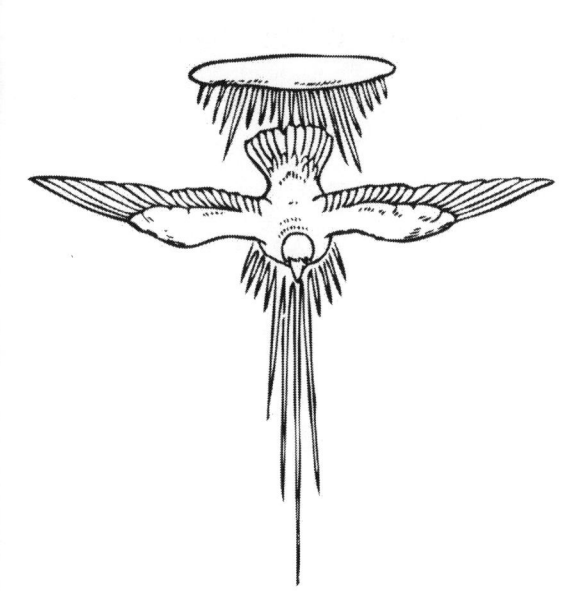

BODY, SOUL & SPIRIT

Mark 12:30, You shall love the Lord with all your heart, your soul, Mind and strength.

I wonder if any of us really grasp the depth of what it means to be saved. Upon salvation most of us experience some spiritual sensation. It may fill us with joy, which may last for a long time or maybe just a moment. But most of us would admit something significant happened. But what really did happen?

We may all understand the fact that through the actions of Adam and Eve we are a fallen race. We may understand that Jesus Christ died on the cross to redeem us from our fallen state. The Word says in John, "for God so loved the world that He gave his only begotten son, that whosoever believes in Him should not perish but have everlasting life." Then He follows with, "God did not send his son to condemn the world, but that the world through Him, might be saved." Now I think I understand the need to be saved, but saved from what. So I ask why?, what is going to happen if I am not saved. In Matthew 8:12 says "the sons of this kingdom will be cast out into outer darkness, there will be weeping and gnashing of teeth. In Matthew 25: 41 says, "depart from Me, you cursed into the everlasting fire prepared for the devil and his angels." Other scriptures paint a different picture of hell itself, but none of it is good. So salvation is a very positive thing, it gives us eternal life, life after death. Now the question is, what internally did salvation do to me? Or what got saved?

When we begin to dig into our human anatomy, we see it is separated into three parts, body soul and spirit. Now in Acts 16 when the jailer asks what must we do to be saved, Peter says, believe in the Lord Jesus Christ and you shall be saved and thy house. So in truth you can't earn it, its a free gift, just believe. Then in Luke 10:25 a lawyer asks what shall I do to inherit eternal life, and in response the answer was, you shall love the Lord your God with all your **heart,** with all your **soul**, with all your **strength** and with all your **mind**, and your neighbor as yourself.

Now as we study these three parts of the human anatomy, the body, soul and spirit, we understand when Jesus poured out his spirit and saved us, it affected our heart. 2 Cor: 5-6 Paul says we preach Jesus Christ, for God commanded light to shine out of darkness who has shone in our heart to reveal God in the face of Jesus Christ. 2 Cor:1:22 says, who has sealed us and given us the spirit in our hearts. So our eyes are open to spiritual things because my heart has been changed, This brings us into re lationship with Him. But we still need to deal with the soul and the body. Now the soul is the mind, where decision are made, where we make choices as to what we are going to do in a situation. Then the flesh or body carries out the orders the soul has commanded. God dealt with the spirit but the soul and body still needs to be addressed.

Now our mind (or soul) has already been programed to the ways of this world. Before we were saved our lives centered around the big "I". Our major concern was me and mine, we valued money, looks, power, prestige and so on, our life's values programmed us to accomplish these things according to the values we held dear. So what we see happening is, when God saved me and gave me his spirit, this action put me out of sink with my pre-programmed mind. Once my spirit was restored or in alignment to God everything changed, and now we begin a lifelong process of re-programing our mind to come into alignment with the Word of God, or heart.

Salvation or going to heaven was instant and free, but

soul saving is a work in progress. Now we can see, God's expectation is for us to love God with all our heart, soul, strength and mind, when you do that you will respond by loving your neighbor. We can know this is the goal God has in mind for us when He saved us as scripture says "you will know them by their love." God's expectation is for us to be transformed so that we may love one another as He has loved us. So this journey is all about removing the big "I" in our lives and replacing it with loving God and your neighbor.

Now we have only the body to think about, but that is simple, as the body is dumb, it only obeys what the mind or soul commands it to do. So as the soul is transformed so will the actions of the body.

GODS GENTLE CONVICTION

John 16:7-11 When the Holy Spirit has come He will convict the world of sin.

As you read this book, it won't take long to recognize that so much of what I say has to do with getting right with God. That's of course because if our spirit is right with God through salvation then it is only the soul that needs to be addressed. Once the soul or mind is in right relationship with God the body will follow, because the body is dumb, it only obeys.

Which reminds me of an experience I had many years ago. When I was young I attended a social function. A bunch of us girls were gathered together and one of our friends name came up, we'll call her Jane. We all added our two cents worth about Jane's shortcomings, not just things we knew, but what we thought we knew. On the way home I heard a voice say, boy you really crucified Jane didn't you! I was cut to the core, God was convicting me of gossip. Now to be honest, I really never thought of myself as being a gossip, I was really shocked at my behavior. Time went on, and I was invited to another social function where many of the same women were gathered. Once again someone's name came up and I found myself chiming in just like the rest, when all of the sudden I remembered! Oh God I'm doing it again, so I did my best to back out of the conversation and say things like however --this, and however-- that, trying to redeem myself for what I had said. At a later function when the women began their chatter, I got up and sat with someone else. When God begins to convict you of a sin in your life, He will continue to press you until you have overcome the sin. Now there is a difference between conviction and feeling guilty, conviction is from God, and it pierces your heart. Acts 2: 37 (At Pentecost) when they heard this they were cut to the heart.

When you feel guilty it affects your heart and mind and is usually from satan just to make you feel bad, then you start beating yourself up, but there's no redemption in it. It is so interesting to me that God cares about our conduct and will so gently bring conviction on you when you least expect, conviction opens my eyes and makes me want to change, I confess but more then anything I want to change, and I am truly sorry for my actions.

Becoming purified is a long process, but the end result is worth it, and when God begins to work on a certain weakness He will pursue it until you have the victory.

CULTIVATING GOOD HABITS

1 Thess.5:11 Therefore comfort each other and edify one another.

One day I read a book by a woman named Arlene Frances, she had written a book called "That Certain Something." I was in my early twenties and it was one of those self improvement books. One of the subjects she addressed had to do with the comments we make. She was stating the fact that your words can build up or tear down a person. The point she wanted to make was, that you can always find something good about people if you make an effort. She pointed out that your comment can have a far reaching effect, such as if you tell a child she has pretty hands, the girl will spend the rest of her life making an effort to display her hands for people to see.

I took her words to heart and made an effort to practice what she taught. Its been fifty years plus now but I still work on building people up. One day as I was in a department store driving one of those little carts, I saw a lady from the back and could see she wasn't young, but she looked nice. I drove my little cart around to face her from the front and said," lady, you know most people have a hard time looking good from the front, but you even look good from the back." Well you can be sure that made her day.

Romans 10:14 let the little children come unto me, and do not forbid them for such is the Kingdom of God.

When I was a Pastor, I started a little group in the church, we called it, "adopt a child." We posted all the children's pictures on the wall with a little bit of information about each of them. The adults were to sign their name under one of the children's names and adopt them for one year. They were asked not to buy expensive gifts for them, but find ways to encourage them. They were to touch them on the arm or head or back and tell them something good like, my what a pretty dress you have on, or how nice your hair looks, or you have such a nice smile. They were asked to do their best to develop a relationship with them. We had some ragged children on our midst, but they all got adopted and the congregation took to heart how important it is to build up these children. I know it had a far reaching effect on the children. That's part of what God calls us to do, reach out, build people up. I have done it so long it has become a habit, and for the most part, I get built up probably more then the one I'm intending to built up.

This story brought back a lot of memories and really hit home for me. As a child in the forty's it wasn't common for adults to converse with children. We truly were seen and not heard. I can remember attending Church and Sunday School every Sunday, then again on Wednesday night, and I don't remember a single adult saying a word to me with the exception of a woman asking me if I would like to be baptized. The conversation was so out of the normal that I still remember where I stood, and the fact the sun was shinning bright. It's like children lived in a vacuum, strangely I walked 3/4 mile to church and back, that same woman who asked me to be baptized lived just down the road from me and never once did she offer me a ride. But to be honest there were at least four other families who passed me on their way to the same church and that covered a twelve years period. The truth is we need to get out of ourselves and acknowledge others if we intend to be a follower of Christ, and children desperately need to be acknowledged.

FORMULA FOR SIN

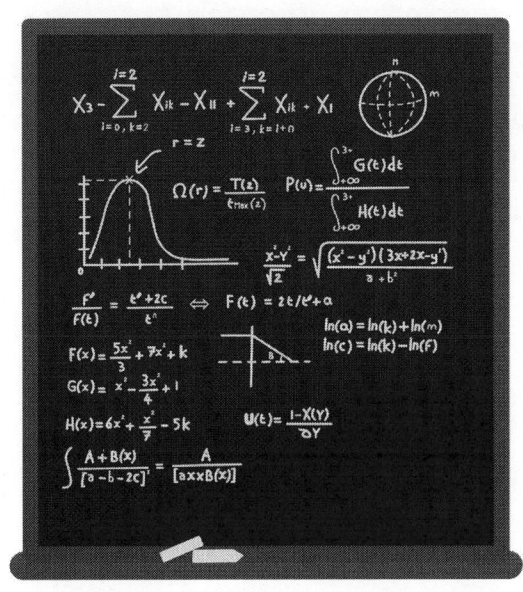

Proverbs 23:7 So as a man thinketh, so is he.

In Genesis we read of God's handiwork in the creation of the earth including the formation of man. Once man was created he gave him two simple directives, first Genesis 2:16 "now God said, you may eat freely of every tree in the garden," followed by the second," however, "one tree you may not eat of, and that is the tree of the knowledge of good and evil." One yea and one nea. Simple and to the point. Yet we know what happened next.

Now lets read on for a descriptive breakdown as to how it happened. Genesis 3:6 "So when the woman saw that the tree was good for food; that it was pleasant to the eyes; and the tree desirable to make one wise, she took of its fruit and did eat."

Now how could she get caught up so quickly in that trap. Lets look more closely. She "saw," one might get the impression that it wasn't just a quick glance, we might even consider the fact that she was somewhat captivated by the apple, after all she looked long enough to see that it would have been good enough to eat.. enter in choices, decisions. Then it goes on to say, it was pleasant to the eyes, this shows she was contemplating, evaluating. At this point she takes it a little farther, desirable to make one wise, in other words, she now sees there is even more value to this apple then just the actual taste, it may have the capacity to make one wise. She reaches out and causes sin to enter mankind. Little did she know the consequences of her sin.

Here we see the formula for sin. It is in the looking. We can see an apple, but if we look away we will be safe, but it is in the looking steadfast that gets us into trouble. One cannot prevent opportunities to "see sinful things," a practically naked lady, lets face it, the billboards are on every corner. A valuable object out of place and available. It is not the seeing that's the sin, it's the continued look or studying of the object. You will never sin if you don't allow yourself to study the possibility. Oh, you have no intention of course, but if you keep looking sin will enter your mind and it becomes a possibility.

Now I'm no student of the human anatomy, but has been explained to me by someone who is, that when you see something, it goes into your computer (brain) and responds that this is new, a first time object is then programed into your brain, now if you have seen it before it is discharged from the brain because its already in there. However, if you continue to look at it, so as to contemplate on it, it goes to the back part of your brain and then into your heart. Let me give you an example. You see a naked person, you look away, your brain says you've already seen one anyway. You look away it's gone. However, if you continue to look, it goes to the back of the brain and then into the heart. Now you may not act on it, but now it's there in your heart, and when an opportunity arises you may consider acting on it. You can be sure satan will take advantage and bring the image and thought up at every opportunity. It is the same with any kind of sin. It's what you think or contemplate on, that gets into your brain and then into your heart. That's why Jesus works so hard to purify the heart. He says it's out of the heart that man sins.

    I'm not crazy about sharing this experience, but it happened and is true. After my husband died, I made up my mind to be done with men, and would live alone the rest of my years. Now I watched a little TV, but now and then I would watch a program, or see an ad that often showed sexual images. Then at night I would have lewd dreams, things that I would never even have thought of. I come to realized they were the result of something I had seen on TV. So I learned to look away at any picture that had any sexual content. Well that's about impossible, so I quit watching TV for awhile and the dreams went away. Now I am very cautious about what I watch and quickly flip the channel if necessary.

Your heart is the judgement seat. A pure heart is the focus of true spirituality. I am not just talking about the physical body but any kind of sin. The control is the decision not to look on anything that will tempt you, alcohol, cigarettes, opposite sex, stealing, you name it. We have the formula for sin laid out by Eve, and God has been generous enough to spell it out for us.

Window peepers become rapists, speed kills, egging someone on to smoke destroys not only the pocket book, but their lungs. Looking at the opposite sex and letting your mind ponder the wrong thoughts, destroys marriages. The world is full of temptation, but if we cast out the first thought, and learn to look away, we will live a healthier life. Stop; look; and listen may be good to prevent a train accident, but it is devastating to the human soul.

EFFECTIVE CHRISTIANS

Philippians 4:8 Finally Brethern, whatsoever things are true, whatsoever things are honest, whatsoever things are pure; just; or of good report, think of these things.

The difficulty of spiritual life is to think on the Word against the reality of the flesh. Dr. says you are sick, Word says you are healed. It is a big challenge, that is why it is so difficult when someone says they are a good Christian when all they are is a good church goer who has learned to do a few nice things. Spiritual life is walking the Word so when the world hits you, you have the spiritual powers to combat it.

The Church does not prepare us for walking the Word, it's just--come to church; do good; and tithe.

The church has so failed the body of Christ. When people get sick they remember some scripture that addresses that topic and begin to claim a healing. It doesn't work that way. We are to be transformed into a spiritual being applying the Word of God to all aspects of our life, so we can reveal the true love of God as well as the power of God. In the end we are to be the light of Christ.

BECOMING AN OVERCOMER

1 Thessalonians 5:8 Praise God for all things.

In the earlier pages of this book, I shared how divorce was not even in my vocabulary. Unfortunately that did not prove to be true for me. I had been married twenty years and had three wonderful boys. Things had been pretty rough between my husband and I for the past year or more. However, we still went on two or three day wonderful vacations up to the dunes at Lake Michigan. The water was warm and the waves were wonderful. We camped out and had many wonderful friends that joined us each trip.

I had just finished reading a book while on the way up north to the dunes. It proclaimed we were to learn to praise the Lord in all things, not just when things went well, but even when they were not. It was a powerful book that made the argument, that praise opens a channel for God to move into even the most dire of circumstances.

When I had a break from setting up camp I decided to take a long walk along the beautiful sandy beach. I had gotten to the point I loved my privacy and the opportunity to pray. But then something happened between my husband and I that pulled the rug out from under me, it was a devastating experience, and crushed me to the bone. At this point all I could do was start walking down the beach, the tears welling up within me, my heart felt as though it had been torn out of my body. I walked for a long time, confused and broken, when I remembered the book. Praise me in all things. Even now Lord! should I praise you now? I stood there ankle deep in water, looking across the endless body of water and grit my teeth, and while tears fell off my cheeks, I began to praise the Lord and I kept on praising. I don't really know how long, but all of the sudden a peace came over me so powerful that I was set free from the pain. I knew in my heart that things would all work out. Praise opened the door for peace.

Now from the moment I was Spirit filled my greatest desire was to serve God, I prayed daily for it and begged God to open the door but it never seemed to happen. As time went on my husband and I were eventually divorced.

Then, many years later, I Had the opportunity to serve God by becoming a Pastor. I went to Garrett Theological school at Northwestern University in Evanston Illinois, just north of Chicago, which is on the West side of Lake Michigan.

Now when I am near water I just have this urge to put my feet in, but on the west side of the lake where I was at there is no beach just gigantic rocks. I climbed down the rocks and finally put my feet in the water. Just then the spirit spoke to me, remember when you were on the other side of the lake, with tears rolling off your cheeks, I am now answering your prayer to serve me. It was such a powerful experience. God is faithful.

We don't know what our tomorrow is going to be, but if we are faithful to God He will make a way where there is no way. He will fulfill the desires of your heart.

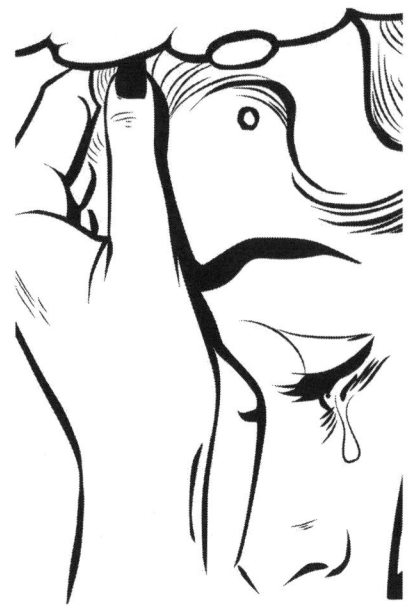

DIVORCE

Since divorce is such a common thing today, I will share a few things that happened to me. First I might add, I have always said it takes two to make it and two to break it, and I take my share of the responsibility in my own divorce. Divorce is one of the most devastating things that can happen to a family. Not only does it destroy the two who are going through it, but the children really get the brunt of it. Then it's terribly painful for the two sets of grandparents, so you might think twice before you take that step.

In the process of our breakdown my husband moved out for a few weeks. We had three boys, nine, twelve and thirteen and we lived in a very nice house in an area that was on the river, and somewhat in the country. While he was gone the boys went to mow the lawn and we couldn't get the mower started. What a bummer, where is your man when you need him. A few days later my youngest wanted to build a little wooden house for the cat. I attempted to help him but no carpenter am I. It really made me realize how these boys needed their dad. Much later when the breakdown was imminent I read an article that said, kids don't care which parent they live with, as long as they can be in their home. I knew if I got custody of the boys I would never be able to afford the house, and we would end up in some old rental in town. I had no job at the time. But he was a good provider, as well as a good father. He had all the skills to teach the boys electrical, mechanics and the works. I knew I needed to move out and leave them with their dad.

We got joint custody and we made sure we kept in close relationship. He didn't make decisions about the boys without discussing it with me, and I got the boys anytime I wanted them.

He re-married very soon, and though it took some time to get over the humps, we stayed friends through it all. I was always seeking the Lord and trying to be obedient to Him and doing all that I could God's way, and yes, even in divorce God stays with you. God hates divorce, but He loves each person and was faithful as He walked me through it all. One of the things I needed to do was to forgive...it takes time, but I did forgive.

One night I was sobbing over not having my boys, when out of the blue God said to me, Mary, all parents have to leave their children sometime, you just had to do it a little earlier then most. Once again I had peace in the midst of the storm.

I might add that he and his wife were married twenty five years, and I was now a Pastor. When she died he asked me to do her funeral and I did, and when he died I did his as well. God calls us to be overcomers. We also know that scripture reminds us we never walk alone. Thru it all, thru it all, I've learned to trust in Jesus, I've learned to trust in God, thru it all, thru it all, I've learned to depend upon His word.

NEW BEGINNINGS

Luke 6:38 Give, and it will be given to you; good measure, pressed down, shaken together and running over will be put into your bosom. For with the same measure you use, it will be measured back to you.

In 1961 my husband and I decided to join the church. We went through several classes of instruction, and when we were finished we made the commitment to join. Then the Priest asked us how much did we want to donate to the church. Donate to the church! I was so ticked off, just like the stories go, join the church so they can get into your pocket. I looked at my husband and he looked as bewildered as I was, so I shrugged my shoulders and said to the Priest, two dollars I guess, so we signed the pledge for that amount. Every week I would write out our check for two dollars. About a year later they had a man give a testimony; he was from Detroit and had ten children. He talked about how much he had been blessed by tithing ten percent of his income. He said scripture tells us in Malachi 3:10 "Bring in all the tithes into the storehouse, that there may be food in my House and prove Me now in this, says the Lord of hosts, if I will not open for you the windows of heaven and pour out for you such a blessing that there will not be room enough to receive it."

Now even though I was quite well versed in the Bible, I had missed the message of tithing. So this all came as quite a shock, were supposed to tithe? Really? The mans message really stirred my soul and I felt convicted to increase our giving, I ask my husband if we could give ten dollars next week. Now ten dollars surely wasn't ten percent of our income, but to me it was a big step. I can still feel the apprehension as I wrote out that check ten dollars. Now wouldn't you know it, before that week was over we got this check from an insurance company for over three hundred dollars we didn't even know we had coming. I remember thinking wow, it does work, this is amazing.

As my relationship grew in Christ, my giving continued to grow until I was faithful in tithing.

I have had so many experiences regarding tithing I could almost write a whole book about the subject, but there is one thing I would like to share. Recently I have been mentoring a young lady and she said, "I don't understand, why does God care about money, what difference does it make to Him." I told her about the scripture where God says to cast you bread upon the waters and it will come back ten fold, as well as other scriptures. But that didn't answer her question.

Now I learned about tithing through this mans testimony, but I grew in my understanding through the teaching of Oral Roberts. He taught me the principles of tithing and increased my knowledge of scripture. But I too had the question, why does it matter to God.

I came to realize, it is the only tangible way God can show us that He cares for us and is vested in our life. As we give, we see God respond so generously, we begin to think, God is there, maybe God does care, maybe He really means what He says. This is the beginning of faith. It is a visible way where God can prove that He is faithful, and His word is true. It is one of the most powerful acts of God. When I see God's faithfulness in tithing I am convinced He loves me, His word is true, this enhances my relationship with Him. Now I am more apt to step out in faith in some of His other promises.

FAITH

Faith is the built up confidence, you have established in something.

Lets say you weigh 300 pounds, you visit a house and you eye all the chairs, which one will hold me! You've been in enough chairs to know they don't all hold you, so you are very conscious where you sit. Then you see one, its just like the one you've sat in before without any problems so you have "faith" it will hold you. Trial and error, you've had to take a chance. Once you've had success in a chair it is no longer chance, but confidence or "faith."

In Christ we find an area to work in to build up faith. There's a multitude of areas, healing; finding a job; salvation; trusting a person, who to marry. That's why I push tithing so much, as I've said before. Tithing gives you the quickest response in building your confidence in Christ. It is the most tangible. First you've got nothing to loose but a few dollars. You give a few bucks, oops it comes back so quick. You try it again, wow, you got a return already. You are now building up a confidence by establishing it in tithing. In time you may trust God in something else, just because you see His faithfulness in tithing.

CHANCE

When we are new in Christ it seem our eyes are open to so many new things, and one of the most threatening is the word faith. People push it on you, just have faith, God is faithful, and so on, but you just come up out of the water and faith ain't an easy lesson. Lets face it the world has opened my eyes, I'm not stupid, I've learned not to pick up hitch-hikers for a reason, I've learned not to trust, oh I'll give it right back, yea, I've heard it all, I'll be right back, "it won't hurt", no really, it won't hurt. Give me a break, I didn't wake up yesterday. So "just have a little faith in Jesus," are not words that come easy.

We are switching from a tangible world to an intangible world. A world of "black and white" to a world of "pie in the sky." The world of physical reality and a world of spiritual reality are both reaching out saying trust me.....but I need a reason. That's right, why should I step out in the blind and take a chance on something. Or I might just say, why do I need faith? Well I could take you right back to your salvation, why did you bother? Number one, someone convinced you there is a heaven and your not going there without a change of heart. The Holy spirit spoke to your heart and you accepted the truth of the gospel and repented from your sin and received Jesus Christ as your savior.

Well its like the Visa card, wow by getting the visa card you just took advantage of getting a few cents back on every dime you spend...but that's not all, you now have free access to air flights, and cruises and a multitude of other things... Well congratulations, because by being saved you now have access to a world way beyond your comprehension, and I can't wait for you to start using you "salvation card." Yes this card covers, healing for your body; financial enhancements; favor; baptism of the Holy spirit; deliverance ; you are no longer under the law now, but grace; supernatural power; wisdom, discernment, forgiveness, knowledge, oh the list goes on... Welcome to my world. Ya get it!

You took a chance on getting saved, and if you are like most, the first reality was that sense of freedom, you actually felt something, a peace came over you,..you say to yourself, there is something to this isn't there. Now that is just the beginning, because like the visa card, you opened a new door to a new life that is incredible. Everything you do now is taking **chances**, until you become so convinced that by taking a **chance** on the word of God it is **no longer a chance**, you know whatever the cry, God will be there. Yes, there is a return on this card and it gets bigger every day. Taking that chance opens the door to faith, and faith opens a door to a new and better world.

FORGIVENESS AGAIN

It is interesting to note how difficult it is to measure Spiritual growth. I used to ask my husband about every six months, do you see a change in me, am I more patient, do I have more peace etc. There some aspects of spiritual maturity that you never know if you have reached a level of maturity at all. I've been Spirit filled forty eight years and still wonder if I have any wisdom, then out of nowhere someone will say, my that was a wise response. However, there is one spiritual move that gets quick response and that is forgiveness.

Forgiveness is one of the biggest stumbling blocks in spiritual growth. There are many people who come to a screeching halt because they cannot forgive. They skirt around it and try to move on, but always they fail to grow in maturity. They so often end up in bondage, become extremely depressed and don't understand why. I've counseled many many people with this issue, and for some reason they don't get it. I do know there are times when they make an effort to forgive, but their heart is so hard, they can't get past the problem.

Lets look at this closely. Jesus says repent of all your sin and accept Jesus Christ as your savior and He will give you salvation. There are no words to describe the freedom we receive when we do that. We know the Word says, by His strips He has set us free and by His blood we are healed. So here we are totally free from every sin we put under the blood. But then the Lord's prayer tells us to forgive others as He has forgiven us. Most of us would say that sounds like a fair deal, after all He forgave me, didn't cost me a thing, However, many people have a big problem with forgiveness.

Most of us would say well shame on you, how can you be so selfish, but in truth there are good reasons why it's hard to forgive. In truth it boils down to "my rights." There are situations that give me the right to not forgive, and lets look at why. Someone abused my child, or kidnapped them, or was drunk and killed my husband, son or family member. Violence that has destroyed loved ones and left permanent damage. We live in a violent world and there are many unjust things happen to people and you can't blame them for not forgiving.

Let me remind you of the first lesson on kingdoms.

In this world that Satan has control of we expect justice, we have rights, an eye for an eye, it is a natural response, we are designed or programmed to quickly react to anything that affronts us. In this natural world we certainly cannot be judgmental about anyone failing to forgive a horrendous deed.

But not in the Kingdom of God. Lets look at it this way, your child was sexually molested and it really destroyed her life. Justifiable, you have hate in your heart, because you can't take it away. You can't set her free, you have a right to hate, your broken. But that hate in your heart builds up and in truth changes your personality. Your don't trust people anymore and so on. It has made you ugly on the inside, and whether you like it or not, it will come out through you in a variety of ways. Violent things change people permanently and for the most part it grows and grows. That's exactly what Satan wants, keep things stirred up. Let there be no unrest or peace. Now what does that hate in your heart get you? It doesn't effect the person you hating at all, it only effects you.

Now I can understand the feeling you have, believe me I've been down the road myself, so I know the challenge.

But lets look at the spiritual aspect of this situation. Unforgiving binds people. Think of a triangle made of rope. God on the top point, and you on the one bottom point and the one your hating on the other bottom point. Hate has the rope pulled tight. You pray and pray for some justice, some relief, but it doesn't come, the reason is, as long as you hate, you keep the rope tight and God can do nothing. But if you make even the slightest effort to forgive, you loosen the rope and you set God free to help you find peace and or justice. "What you bind on earth is bound in heaven, what you loose on earth is loosed in heaven." Scripture   Matthew 18:18

    Peace only comes when you are willing to let go. You may have to start slowly. Maybe by saying God help me, I want to let go, I know this unforgiving is eating me up and I want to let go, but I can't. Help me to be willing. If you pursue this attitude there will come a moment, when you will realize the hate is gone. Your hate isn't changing a thing in the culprit who did this, but if you let go God can nail the person and bring some peace. There is no justice in some situations but there can be peace and healing, so you can go on. God didn't tell us us to forgive others as he forgave us because he wants attention, or blind obedience, but because He knows hate destroys us, God loves us and wants us free.

SPIRITUAL GROWTH

If I were to say one spiritual walk is a cut above another, I would say there is a reason for that. I'm nearly 80 years old, I've been saved since I was five and filled with the Spirit since I was 30. At 5 the advantage, of which I wasn't aware of, was every Bible story built my faith in God, I never questioned anything I heard spiritually. The story of Daniel and lions den, the story of Joseph and his coat of many colors, Jesus walking on the water, you name it and I knew it was true. So when I became totally sold out and filled with the Spirit at 30 I had a good foundation. I built on that foundation with determination. I read everything I could get my hands on. I never questioned that what-ever experience happened to the person in the book, was something I could expect if I got that far spiritually. I read the latest books that were out, and that was considerable, as there was a move of the Spirit in the early 70's and men like Merlin Carothers, and the men of that era were all putting it all down on paper. Then I read the old goodies, books from Spiritual movements that happened in the 1800 and up, I read many books on St. Augustine, St. Frances and others. I filled my head with the knowledge of God. I saw no reason why anything that happened to them couldn't happen to me, "God is no respecter of persons."

The next brick in my foundation was prayer, I had a prayer list a mile long, but beside that I praised God endlessly, I sought him as though he were in the room with me. He was never a distant God you can't touch or say some things to, for some reason, I never set God aside as some Holy creature I couldn't communicate with. I talked to him like he was my best friend.

After I was spirit filled for a few months, I sought after the gift of tongues. A polite way of begging, begging endlessly, demanding! "your Word says" God I'm calling you on this, oh I was bold, if His word says it then I believed it and He better come through. I'm not saying that's right or wrong, but I think He liked my boldness, because He came through and the spirit just poured through me like rushing water. I was afraid to go to bed at night, because I was afraid it would be gone in the morning. Well guess what... it was gone, all I had left was "scutta, dutta, do" I was crushed, but not without hope. I had "scutta dutta do" for a week or two and would always say it in my prayer. Then one day I decided I would press God a little further and say scutta, dutta, do for ten solid minutes. That may sound easy, but try it sometime, ten minutes seemed like hours. But I made up my mind, and when I did, God just poured out His spirit on me, I not only spoke in the spirit but I also sang in the spirit with a voice I didn't even know I had. I worshiped Him for hours. Perseverance my dear, perseverance, show God you mean it, and you'll do anything you have to to get closer to Him. I have had a wide variety of languages every since, either in song or word, and I rarely pray in my own english language. Why, you say. Well I'm glad you asked!

Romans 8:26 "Likewise the spirit helps us in our weakness, for we do not know what to pray for as we ought, but the Spirit Himself intercedes for us with groaning to deep for words."

Ephesians 6:18 "praying at all times in the Spirit, with all prayer and supplication."

Jude 1:20 "But you beloved, building yourselves up in your most holy faith and praying in the Holy Spirit."

1 Cor. 14:15 "What am I to do? I will pray with my spirit, but I will pray with my mind also, I will sing with my Spirit, but I will sing with my mind also."

Aren't the Words of God beautiful. He calls us deeper, don't listen to people around you who are content with a splash of the Spirit, go for the gold.

Spiritual growth comes through a consecrated effort, because of a hunger in your heart. It is rarely just dumped on you, you work for it.

Lastly - the final effort on my part was fasting. I don't know where it was introduced to me, but I took it to heart and began to study up on the subject. I first got a book that addressed the physical aspect of fasting. When that book showed me fasting was not only good for the spiritual life, but exceptional for the physical, I was sold. Who couldn't use a boost in both the physical and spiritual? One thing that came through to me was a fast means just that, no food. For the physical benefits, it's not a fast unless it is a total fast. There are other ways of doing things like just juice etc, but that's not what the pro's call a fast. A fast for health benefits are no food, and that works the same for the spiritual fast. If your going to do it, get serious and do it right. Now there are many forms of discipline, you may want to put your body through, no coffee, or just coffee, no sweets, or no meat, whatever, but don't play games, either do it and expect a spiritual response or don't do it. But if your working toward being a spiritual power house then get real and fast. The benefits are enormous, there is power in fasting, and when you include serious prayer you can move mountains.

I want to share the story of my latest fast, I was living in LasVegas working with drug addicts when my son encouraged me to move to North Carolina. I did and I got an apartment near where he lived. He decided he wanted a little help with the bookkeeping of his business and so I spent a few hours each week helping him. He had a drinking problem, but during work hours kept it under control. He had made a commitment to God some years previously and was baptized and all that, so I knew he knew God and even went to church occasionally and tithed. But in the last many months he had lost his way and was really being challenged with his drinking. He was forty years old and never married. Now every time I would go to his place, God would whisper in my ear, your going to live here! For a solid year God would tell me that. Finally I said, darn it God if he wants me to live here then he's going to have to ask me. Now I did not desire to live where he lived or with him. The following Monday there was a knock on my door and it was my son, Mom I'd like you to come live with me, and he had his reasons. I told him I had just signed another years lease and there's no way it can happen now. Well try and see if you can get out of the lease. So I went to the manager and asked. Now some time previously the manager's mother had cancer and I had prayed over her. Her cancer went away, and in the end, the manager gave me the credit, now I know better, but to go on. Because of that she told me she would relieve me of the lease. Wow. 'God makes a way when there is no way."

When I moved in with my son, I had one end of the place to myself, but I knew God had me there for one reason, I was to be his covering, that means he's under my spiritual umbrella. I knew God was after the drinking, but I never! never! in the whole year I lived there, said one word about his drinking. I went into overtime prayer and I fasted one day a week. My fast was no food from Sunday night till Tuesday morning, a 36 hour fast with just water. He was dating a woman who personally I didn't think was good for him, but I said nothing. Now a series of things happened, he got a ticket or DUI, the woman pulled a nasty thing on him, and he said mom I need to get rid of my drinking, and that night he went to a AA meeting. He hasn't had a drink in a year and a half, he met a sweet woman, married her and they had a baby girl who was a #3 baby but is healthy and happy. God answers prayer!

What really happened, my prayers for him through the years gave God the permission to set it all up. It was the timing of the Lord. When God was ready to move he laid it on my heart to go into overdrive with prayer and fasting. It was all God. When we pray we are giving God permission to work in those we pray for. Remember God does nothing but by prayer.

Philippians 4:6, Be anxious in nothing but in everything by prayer and petition let your request be made know to Him. When you add fasting you are opening that door of possibility far wider, your really giving God the green light. It is so powerful, why people don't get hold of it is beyond me.

WARNING

I want to address a sensitive subject, I would prefer not to, but feel if I am expecting the above written for you to be taken seriously, then I need to make something clear. Lets say you went to a County fair and they had a new ride, you went on it and it was out of this world. Now when you share your experience you share it with enthusiasm, and vigor and excitement. Now lets say the people you shared it with, tell the next person, but it looses it's vigor, it becomes only a fact. If you haven't experienced it there's no inner drive to pass it on. I have been a part of many churches. Catholic, Methodist, non-denominational, and to be honest, it was never in me to be labeled anyone of them. I appreciated them all, but I was always a Christian, worshipping with this or that body of Christ. Now I'm not saying it's good or bad, I'm just saying for me it wasn't the important thing. Now what I have found is that if a Pastor has not spent an hour in prayer every day of the week, or laid prostrate before the Lord on an all night vigil, or made fasting a regular habit, and hasn't experienced the value of those things, he can't pass it on. It's not a value to him, there is no vigor, no excitement of victory in these things because it is not in His experience. You can't give it if you ain't got it. It's only a fact.

The last church I attended, the Pastor would say, it would be a good thing to fast, but then he followed that up with, now if your on medications, or if you want to continue you coffee, or if it's just one meal a day, he gave everybody an excuse not to fast. You know he's not expecting to move a Mountain and has not experienced the value and power of fasting, or he would never put it across the way he did. If you ain't got a preacher who can put the cards on the table and expect you to fast, and expect the Mountain to be moved, then find a preacher who does.

Now the next sensitive fact. Many Pastors, and people in the congregation are often critical of Pastors who have big churches, or do outlandish things. They accuse them of big money, and anything that will be effective in destroying their popularity. Let me tell you something, don't go there. They got thousands of people in their congregation because their passing on the Word. There giving hope, their showing people how to move into a deeper relationship with God. Nobody's going to walk a half mile or so through the parking lot, and wade through a thousand people just to get a seat unless their being fed.

Leaders are jealous, and do their best to reduce them, there's got to be some trick, cause I don't have that many. Well maybe it's because your not preaching the real Word. Let me tell you something, those Pastors have given up everything. Their life is one endless demand. They're sold out on God and His work. So they have the good fortune of being paid a high salary, but don't kid yourself, they sacrifice so much and their families suffer a great deal. Don't begrudge them, they are paying a high price to serve God, and God is blessing them.

Beware of the preacher who just keeps giving you little tidbits. Get a preacher that is pushing you beyond where your at, don't lock out new information if it is in scripture. Theres nothing that has been out lived in scripture, if it's in there, it's for you, all of it. Press on.

PART TWO

GOD'S CHOSEN

Matthew 20:1-15

"For the kingdom of heaven is like a landowner who went out early in the morning to hire laborers for his vineyard. In the first group he agreed to pay the laborer's a denarius a day, about the third hour he hired more laborer's and told them he would pay them a denarius a day, in the sixth hour and again in the ninth hour he hired more men to work, and again promised them a denarius a day. At the end of the day they all lined up to get their pay and he paid each one, regardless of how long they worked, a denarius. When the men who had labored all day saw what was happening they supposed they would get more for they had worked all day compared to those who had worked only a few hours, but they only received a denarius. They murmured to the landowner, "that's not fair." The land owner said, friend I am doing you no wrong, did you not agree to work for a denarius a day. Is it not lawful for me to do as I wish with my own things.

Jesus then says, so the last will be first and the first last, for many are called, but few chosen.

Now the point of this story in Matthew is that God is letting us know that He has the right to call anyone into the Kingdom whenever and however he pleases, it's not on a first come first served basis. Now I don't really know what he means when He says many are called, but few are chosen. I honestly believe He calls most of us if not all of us, but we don't all respond, but that's another story. However, I would like to share something that happened recently, and it refers to the chosen.

THE CHOSEN FEW

My sister-in-law died six months ago, and left a fifty-three year old daughter who was mentally challenged and lived with her mom all her life. Her mother had a reverse mortgage on the house, so after a short time the mortgage company notified the daughter the house will be sold, and she is to get out by such and such a date. Well, I really did not know just how limited the young lady was, but as time got closer to the cut-off date I came to realize she needed help and lots of it.

She needed a place to live, but she had no credit, so no credit rating. She had no bank account and only made $800.00 a month. She was left with nothing monetary from her mother's estate, and only a house-full of figurines her mother had collected, you might say hording style, because there were at least two thousand of them. (nice ones) The daughter was also what you would call a hoarder, she loved animals and had six dogs, four cats, four big birds, four large fish tanks and she collected anything that had an animal on it. Do you have any idea how many cups have dogs on them? and towels, and sheets and...you get the picture.

Now for the past two years I felt the need to help her and her mother with a few dollars on a monthly basis, and felt maybe some how I should help her now. But how? I realized she would have a hard time getting a place to live with no credit, and little income and she didn't have any money to speak of.

Now one day she called and I was having lunch with friends, she begin to tell me of her woes, and I said honey, I'm tied up right now, but I'll call you right back. I started to briefly explain her situation to my friends, when I heard the Lord say, "you go!" Now I'm not an animal lover, particularly in the house, I'm eighty years old, and lived 1200 miles away. But I returned her cry of help and said I will come. However, I had already come to the conclusion she could not possibly afford all her animals, the dogs were all thoroughbred, she keep up with shots and the like and treated her animals very well. But I had to tell her I would help her on the condition she get rid of three of the dogs, and three of the cats, the birds and the fish, because I told her, you just plain can't afford them, and I might add, no apartment complex is going to allow anyone to keep that many animals. She had already been advised of that reality and agreed. In a few days I was on my way. She had also explained to me it was in the 90's and there was no air conditioning. This is Missouri and actually it was 95 degrees everyday for the two plus weeks I was there.

As I was on my way, it came to me, what can I actually do?, I have no strength, I am very limited in my walking, I have a bad heart. Then the Lord spoke to me and said, you are to be the facilitator. Then I thought well ...who would I facilitate because I came to realize my niece would be of little help. But I prayed God, don't let me be overbearing, keep me humble, as it's easy for me to be a take charge person, unfortunately very easy!

Well the second day I was truckin down the road and about to get on a ramp to the main highway when I spotted a hitchhiker, and thought, "why not." "The only thing bad about hitchhikers is that they smell, sometimes pretty bad." I was a hundred miles from Nashville. That's where he was going! Well in conversation he kept bringing up about how the Lord had helped him on several oc casions, but he was now at the bottom of the barrel. I didn't share about my relationship with the Lord at this time. He kept talking and bringing up the Lord and I finally said, you sound like you have a relationship with the Lord. He said he had a little Bible teaching when he was a kid, he was 39 now. He said he had collected probably twenty of those Bible tracks and was carrying them around with him, and for some reason God just kept hounding him. It was at this point I shared with him my own story of my relationship with God. Now as we traveled I kept feeling like I should ask him to go on to Missouri with me, and just when I finally asked him, the Lord said to him "Mission Trip." ...So my new hitchhiker friend and I trucked on to Missouri.

When we got there I let my niece believe I had brought him from home, though I said nothing, and she didn't ask, she received him like a long lost friend, and he also treated her as well. My new friend was magnificent, and this night for the first time in two weeks he had a bed to sleep in.

Well it didn't take long for me to understand I had no concern about being overbearing as my niece was expecting me to take charge, I'm sure due to the pressure she was under she was ready to just let go, help was here, and she was saved by the bell. My friend, I'll call Al and I just got to work, she had found an apartment to live in, but no money to pay the piper, so I dug a little deeper and with the help of a few close family members we got some old bills taken care of, rent paid and also the deposit. My friend Al and I packed a thousand figurines to take to her apartment, as well as many of her other belongings. With her little car and Al's muscle, she was on her way. Never once did he complain, or try to back out, or make an excuse. He was truly the man God designed for 1e to facilitate.

Now I told my niece to put anything she wanted, that she and Al hadn't moved, into her bedroom, because we were preparing for an estate sale, and everything was to go unless it was in her bedroom, including the other thousand figurines. After a week or so of hard work I took my new friend Al to the bus station, gave him a little money and put him on a bus to Nashville. He was such a man of God, I literally expected him to grow wings and fly away when I dropped him off. Then I prepared for the sale. Normally an estate sale brings in a lot of people, but to make this story a little shorter, the truth is four people came, and in total we made two hundred dollars, that was with the 55 Elvis plates, still in their boxes, and the bear rug. But none of the very nice figurines. Then God sent a woman. She could see what I was dealing with, my niece, and the whole situation, she saw my dilemma. The lady said I think I can get you a buyer for the whole thing as these are nice figurines. I said I'll sell the whole bunch for $600.00.

Now it happened my niece's TV had broken two days previous to moving, and ten minutes before the guy came to move the dryer, it broke, so I knew we needed money to replace those two items. The next morning this angel God sent, brought a woman who bought everything in the house my niece didn't want. I put that money in my hot little hand and she and I got into the car and bought her a new TV and a dryer, she also got rid of three cats, four big birds, and all the fish tanks, but only one dog.

The other two will be going soon, well maybe, all this in just two weeks. She is now a happy camper in a lovely apartment, with all of her belongings as well as being closer to her work. What a mighty God we serve!

Now I want to refer back to Matthews Gospel referring to the chosen.

Here is a girl who doesn't have a clue of what a relationship with God is. I have no idea where she stands with God or if she comprehends who Jesus is, yet God called an eighty year old limited woman, to drive 1200 miles, pick up a hitch-hiker, bring us both to her door, sort out all of her 53 years of possession's plus her mom's, bring us a buyer for her "stuff" on the very day we needed one, and then get her in an apartment, with money left over to have one of her dogs groomed. In all my years of walking with God I've never seen such a series of events that God put in place for someone who is oblivious to the whole thing. Surely this typifies a "chosen" child of God.

Now I want to add to the story a little bit of insight. If I were not totally sold out for God, I would have never heard him say "you go." If I would have totaled up my abilities, I would have never made the trip. If I wouldn't have picked up the hitchhiker, the whole thing would have been a wash. If the TV and dryer had not broken when they did, we would have unnecessarily paid to move two items that would have cost extra money, and then when they broke later, she would not have had the money to purchase them. That dryer literally broke ten minutes before the man came to move it. God opened every door, at just the right moment. Please understand the value of being sold out, and trusting Him. Learn to listen to Him, be in a daily walk with Him, it takes intentional practice, but it is so rewarding in the end.

A DENARIUS A DAY

Now the scripture in Matthew also brings out another lesson I learned. It refers to the men who worked for a denarius a day and grumbled about not getting more because they had worked longer. One day I was in the coffee shop enjoying my tea when one of the girls who works there came and set by me. She was bent out of shape, and fuming like a mad man. I said what's wrong? She said do you know what her boss did? He hired that new girl over there for $12.00 an hour. I've been here a year and he only pay's me $10.00 an hour. Under normal situations I would have agreed with her, how unjust, that mean man! But in an instant the scripture in Matthew hit me. My head wanted to respond in the flesh but my spirit wanted to say well didn't you agree to work for $10.00 an hour when you hired in. Now I didn't say it, but how quickly it came to me. Now where's the lesson in all this. If were living by the world's standard we can cry unjust, unfair, and put up a fuss. But if we are living by the spirit we look at it a bit different.

If you are a child of God do remember we are now living in the kingdom of God, not according to this world's standards. Our lifetime business is to be re-programed into Kingdom thinking. Remember the song I've got a new way of walkin, a new way of talkin--we must be re-programed and begin to think "kingdom living." Now what really is the key to this kind of thinking. What can we gain or learn from all this.

Remember our bottom line is to trust in God and learn to love one another. By accepting the fact that I hired in for $10.00 an hour I can change my attitude towards this new girl. If I do, I cut out envy, jealously, resentment and competitiveness. I may even end up getting a raise. If I hang on to these feeling I'm going to stir up trouble, and treat her poorly. I'm going to be jealous and treat her and the boss with an attitude, then I'm going to be competitive, work hard to show her up and so on. Last of all I'm going to resent her, and those feeling tear me up on the inside. There's no good ending with this kind of thinking, but when I take the attitude that "I did hire in at $10.00 an hour, and the other girl...well, she didn't accept that, smart girl! But the big victory is this. When I'm yielded to God, I go to Him with my problem's. If I'm short in dollars I go to God. I put my trust in Him. Of course I tithe, but I am dependent on Him to meet my needs not the coffee shop owner. God owns the cattle on a thousand hills. This is an area we can begin to trust in Him. I love the freedom of being free of being competitive. I don't have to measure up to anybody's standards. This is a powerful lesson, if we can get free of competition we have made great strides in our Christian walk. This is a good example of "this worlds" thinking. If I were hit with this situation and to be honest I have been, my first reaction would be the normal one, no way Hosea, but thank goodness after walking the walk for many years, I often think, what is God saying to me, have I learned this lesson, is my reaction one where God would look upon me in favor. The truth is I want peace, I'm not better than anyone else, but I'm just as good as anyone else. If I've got a problem I take it to my Father, I don't want stinkin thinkin in my life.

THE STANDARD BEARER

In my years as a child of God I often read the history of the Spiritual greats and I so wanted to be like them. I would often attempt to follow their example and do some of the crazy things they did, like sleep on the floor and so on. Unfortunately, or maybe fortunately I didn't seem to get any real spiritual high's from trying to follow in their footsteps. But there was one thing I did pick up that made a difference in my walk. That was fasting. As you already know I refer to it many times in my stories because it is a part of my spiritual discipline, but I want to share an experience I had many years ago.

We lived in a three-story home. My husband would go to work in the morning and my last two sons would go off to school. I had the whole day to myself. I would go to the third floor and stay there for the better part of the day, "my own little spiritual retreat." I would do a water fast for one to three days, and spend the time seeking God through prayer and the Word. I would do this for three to five days. One day as I was praying I had a vision, all the sudden there were three men before me.

On the left was Abraham, I boldly said to him, what do you have for me, he had a mantle over his arm and gave it to me and said this mantle represents a Standard Bearer, you will be a Standard Bearer for Christ. The middle man was Jesus, and I said, what do you have for me, He reached out his hand and touched my forehead and said, I give you my love for those you will be ministering to, the third man was Moses and he handed me his rod or staff, it was twisted and rough and he said you will minister with this rod. I said why is it so rough and he said those knots represent your suffering, you will minister out of the experiences of your own pain. Well at first I couldn't comprehend it, but I wrote it down as I often did and eventually forgot the experience, now and then something would be said and it would all come back to me.

Now in my church I had a man who I really connected with. He had the responsibility of being the man between the people of God and the Preacher. He stood by me through everything. He was a pain in the neck for many of the congregation because he always challenged the people to stick to the by-laws of the church. He called them into accountability at every turn. He was truly a standard bearer. He paid a big price for his role, but he was a magnificent man of God. I recognized what his role was and supported him in every way. I had forgotten that God had told me I was a standard bearer. But because of the giftedness of that role in me I recognized it in him.

Now ten years later and I retired when I was seventy. I moved away and attended many different churches, but often found the leadership in disarray. Many time's I found the preacher falling very short, and it would just blow my mind. One day after going through some old journals, I read about the vision I had, and realized part of my problem is I'm a standard bearer. It's hard for me to see things out of order, though to be honest, I usually don't say a word about it, but it takes the joy out of attending church. There is a price to pay at being a standard bearer, you are representing Christ and or Christs ways. To be honest, when you have a church out of order they want to stay that way and certainly don't want to be corrected. There is God's way of running a Church and man's way. God does not want to have a church run like General Motors, but by being obedient to God's direction. A standard bearer is a stumbling block to them, and they really don't want you around. Now let us not confuse being critical with being a standard bearer. There are those where nothing lines up with the way they think it should be, that doesn't make them a standard bearer, they just have a critical spirit.

Now many churches follow an order the church was designed to follow when it was established, and it doesn't seem to be the same for all. If they are faithful to that order, it will probably work for them. Unfortunately many churches get in trouble when the leader thinks he's God, instead of being a servant of God, responsible for serving the people of God. He often sees himself as the only person God can speak to or through as far as the direction of the church goes and shuns anyone who challenges his position, particularly a standard bearer. He establishes a board who is designed to support whatever he desires, making it look like he is in order when in fact he is only a dictator. You will find these churches grow to a point and then stay there, they have a constant turnover of people.

Now I have often noticed a church will rarely grow past the spirituality of the Pastor, and if he is the only one in charge, then if someone becomes more mature and more spiritual then the Pastor, the Pastor will shut them out, and most of them leave, because there is no room in the Inn. Now there is a price to pay at being a standard bearer, and unless you are in a leadership position it's best to keep your mouth shut, and or move on. But if you are in a leadership position, then learn to share your thoughts as question's, or you might say, I was wondering if we might consider doing it this way? Learn to phrase your objections without turning the room upside down. I can assure you will have a strong personality and come across aggressive, even though you don't see it. Learn to ask, do you think this is the way God would have us go, or what does the Word say about this. Churches so often want to do things the way the world does them, that's not God's way. Ask them if maybe it wouldn't be a good idea to pray about it and see what God would have us do. You can be very helpful, or you can be a pain in the neck.....your choice. You only have a responsibility if you are in a leadership position! If not, bite your tongue! But if you have an open Pastor who is reasonably subject to the board you can be a Godsend to a church by helping them to keep in line with the will of God.

What does this have to do with fasting. I find most spiritual gifts become mature through spiritual discipline and that includes fasting. Fasting breaks the yoke. Fasting takes away that question is this God's idea or mine? If you do a study of the great men of God, you will find all of them fasted. This is part of the call of God for those who want to fulfill the call of God on their lives and I can assure you being a standard bearer is a responsible position.

THE LOVE OF JESUS

As I reread the vision I looked back on my ministry and recognized another part of the vision that had played out in my life, that was loving people with Jesus love. I worked with drug offenders and alcoholic's for twenty years. I had a class of thirty men in Vegas where I lived for five years. I used to wonder how it was that I never saw their short comings, but always saw their potential and somehow was able to love them unconditionally. It used to amaze me, because I lived with many of them and I knew how they could lie, cheat and steal without batting an eye, but I never stopped loving them. I later realized that was the love Jesus gave me when he touched me in the vision, God's love for the people I ministered to, what a blessing. That love built men up and gave them hope. I didn't need to "work up" love on my part, Jesus had already given it to me. I've have now come to recognize God's love working trough me when it happens. I used to wonder how it is that some drug addicts just bring out such love and understanding through me and others, I have to conjure up all the love I can muster, and bite my tongue. This insight was very advantageous for me because I then questioned if I should take on some of the cases if I don't have His love. I also learned not to take credit for my "sweet spirit" because I know it's not my love, but God's. I don't know if I had remembered the vision during my years of ministry, if it would have made a difference, but regardless, I can tell you what a joy it was to speak to thirty men out of God's love, and to build them up and not hit them over the head because of their lifestyle. It is amazing to be a child of God and to spend your life serving Him, God is so good.

THE PAIN OF LIFE'S CHALLENGES

The last part of the vision became real to me in that I ministered out of my own pain. How true, I've been down the road and suffered many things, but I always seemed to work my way through things with the light of Christ, and because I did, I was able to help others find a way to victory in their pain. God is so faithful.

In the last year I have worked as an Uber Driver. I'm in a college town and serve many young people. Many are at a crossroads in their life and like to share their story. I'm somewhat like a hairdresser, or bar tender, people will share many personal things to strangers. But what an opportunity. I don't tell them I'm a retired Preacher, but take any opportunity I can to share the Word of God. Before I start my car in the morning I pray, God let me be sensitive to each person I pick up, give me discernment, let me know if you want me to share a Word with them. My car is a church on wheels. God brings so many people to me. One of the opportunities I have is when they are disgruntled. I ask them if they know God has a plan for their life, that He created them and all of their intricate parts to fulfill a certain role in society. I also tell them they may work somewhere, but feel like moving on, but when they come to the place God created them for they will be totally happy doing whatever that may be. Believe me it works. People are hungry for a Word, and it's not just the young people. I share any aspect of my life that will build up people. The most effective evangelism is personal story, and most of us have suffered some real setbacks, but those setbacks can help you to share out of your own pain. "Look what God has done for me!"

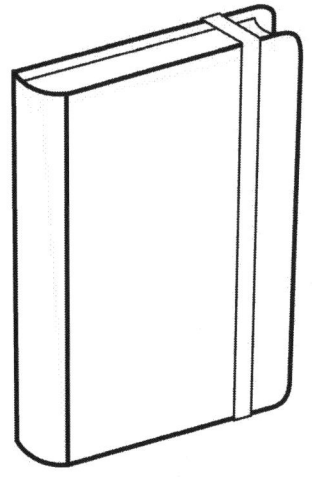

BOTTOM LINE

Now I want to share this to those who are truly sold out for Christ. You may or may not have had a vision, but you may have had a dream, or someone may be talking to you and all the sudden say something you know was from God and the other person won't even know it. Or you may be reading the Bible and something hits you and you know God is speaking to you. I have found people who have cultivated spiritual discipline, will have often heard a word from God. But we often question it because we don't see immediate results from it. Now as I look back I see God works it out in your life and you may not even realize it. When God imparts something in you, it's there and He is faithful to carry it out. I kept a little journal to record the Word when God was speaking to me. It's nice to re-read the journal and find some message He gave me that came to pass and I didn't even realize it until I read it again. I just want to encourage you, God is with you every moment, and he will never fail you. He's with you even when your not with him.

FASTING

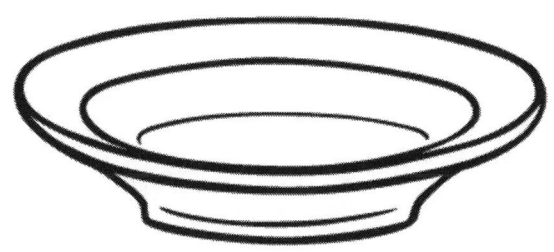

Well I tried to stay away from this message, but since I consider it to be the second most important discipline in my life, I feel the need to share it. When I first began to toy with the idea of fasting, I thought I would check into what the nutritionist had to say about it: OK, Let's see what the nutritionist say about fasting.

I will refer to Dr. Braggs book called "The Miracle of Fasting. He says "we live in a world full of pollution, the air we breathe is full of toxins, the large cities are pumping the air full of smog, a mixture of soot and smoke from factories, the toxic exhaust from cars and trucks, add to the problem. The chemicals in our water, as well as the fertilizer used in growing our plants, continues to add to the problem, these pollutant's are not digestible, they just settle in your body eventually lodging in the tissues and joints for future problems. There is no pill to resolve this build up. Diet drinks and the like are far worse for you then the sugar, because you can digest sugar, but you can't digest the ingredients in a diet food."

"However, a water fast once a week will begin to flush these enemies out of the body and rebuild the vital force needed for every organ in your body to function properly."

Now that is just an overview of what he shares, it is in agreement with many other supporters of fasting. I highly recommend you study up on fasting from a nutritional point of view. Once you are convinced it is physically one of the best things you can do for your body you will never question the spiritual.

Now let's see what the Bible has to say about fasting.

New Testament, Mark 4:1 this is the story of Jesus fasting for forty days, and I'm sure your familiar with this one.

Now in Matt. 6:16 Jesus tells them "when you fast, do not be like the hypocrites, but anoint your head, wash your face so as not to appear to men to be fasting and your father sees in the secret place and will reward you openly." Now that's interesting, "when" you fast, it appears to me he expects his followers to fast!

Mark 2:18, Pharisees ask Jesus why don't your disciples fast, Jesus says, not while the bridegroom is with them, but when He is taken away they will fast.

Luke 3:36 is telling the story of a Godly woman named Anna who served God with fasting and prayer day and night.

In Acts 13:1 The Spirit tells the followers to separate Saul and Barabas for my work, then after fasting and prayer they laid hands on them and sent them away.

Last, 2 Cor:4 But in all things we commend ourselves to the ministry of God, in patience, tribulations, in needs, and fasting.

Now I find it pretty hard to ignore the Word of God in fasting. If we are being called to be a follower of Christ it is vital we fast. We don't need to study scripture to justify the need to pray, why do we ignore the Word on fasting.

Now let me make this very clear. Fasting means going without food and special drinks. There is no place that says do without water. I've heard preacher's say Jesus did not drink water when he fasted, really, show me in the Bible where it says that, I can assure you it is not there. Fasting is with water. Now I boil when I hear a preacher say let's do a 21 day fast, fast however you want to. What does that mean? Oh I'm going to give up coffee, really! or juice, or sweets or meats or whatever, that is a nice sacrifice but it is not fasting. Now I think God is pleased to see you make some small sacrifice, but don't expect

Him to do a great deal because of it, it doesn't work that way.

Well what's the point! First let's look at Jesus fast. He was baptized, and went to the desert to pray and fasted for forty days. Why? What did He hope to accomplish by fasting. So simple, Jesus was God and man, he had the human traits in him as we do, but he fasted to bring those human qualities under control. NOW, he could do just what the Father asked him to do, NOW he had to power to be absolutely obedient to His Father, NOW He could accomplish the job He was sent to do. You ask why do we fast, for the same reason. If you want to get close to God, then fast. Do you have a special need, pump your prayer with fasting. You want to know how God wants you to serve him, add fasting to your prayer. Get serious, what a waste of time to settle for a sprinkle of the spirit. Get saturated, create some spiritual disciplines, live out your life in service to Him.

Now I'm not going to leave it there. I mean, let's face it, there is more and I will do whatever it takes to convince you fasting is one of the most powerful tools God has made available for our walk with Him.

Let's look at the old testament. In Joel we see a prophecy that says," tell the people of God to turn to Me with all you heart, with fasting, with weeping and with mourning."

In Judges we have the Israelites fighting the tribe of Benjamin, and the first day they took a heavy loss, the second day once again they took a heavy loss, then all the people of God went to the house of God and wept, and sat before the Lord and fasted that day until evening, the next day "the Lord defeated Benjamin before Israel."

In 2nd Chronicles 20, several tribes came against Jehoshphat to battle, so Jehoshaphat feared and set himself to seek the Lord, and proclaimed a fast throughout Judah, now all Judah with their little ones and wives stood before the Lord, and the spirit came upon Jahaziel and said, "do not be afraid or dismayed because of this great multitude for the battle is not yours but God's. Through a series of events they went to battle, it turned out an angel had destroyed the enemy and "there were dead bodies fallen on the earth, not one escaped." Because they called a fast!

Now lastly, we see Jonah is told to go to Ninivah and warn the people of coming disaster due to their foul living. In the end the King called the people to fast, not only food, but water as well, and also their animals, and the city was saved. Ninivah is was one of the largest cities in the history of the Bible. The list goes on. Oh, but what about Daniels fast - show me where it says he fasted. Now he went on a vegetarian diet, but it does not say he fasted. Now his long sacrifice of a vegetarian diet with no sweets paid big dividends, but it does not say he fasted. Now I encourage you to look up these scriptures so you can come to understand the power of fasting.

Now let me stretch my luck here. In life many people have the strong desire for sweets, or maybe alcohol, it could be cigarettes. When we have this overpowering desire and just can't seem to overcome it, it is because Satan has lured you into becoming addicted to these killers. I have found when a person begins to set up a serious program of fasting they are taking their life back. Because what happens! you overcome the enemy and get back in charge of your life. A twenty-four hour fast is a great start, if you can go 36 hours that even greater. First start with a 24 hour fast once a week for several weeks and then move to a 36 hour fast. I can assure you, you will reap benefits within weeks not only in your health, but in your spiritual life as well. History records the power of fasting, I've only touched on a few points. I encourage you to get into the Word and look up fasting. You will see the power of God is loosed through fasting. You want your child free of drugs, free of alcohol, free of porn. You want a breakthrough in your life, fast. When accompanied with prayer It is the most effective discipline you can administer to your situation.

THE TRANSFER TO GOD'S KINGDOM

You have heard me refer to moving into God's Kingdom many times. I'm sure it would be nice if I broke that down a little and clear up what it really means.

Let's take a book and put it on the table, now say that book represents the people on earth. Now we know that Satan invaded the people on earth and the kingdom was lost to Him. God lost his cherished possession. All mankind is now vulnerable to influence from Satan, and we are a lost people. A living hell is our promise. Now let's take a cloth and put it over that book, that cloth represents the blood of Jesus and through His blood with the confession of faith we then exit Satan's kingdom and gain entrance to the Kingdom of God. We are delivered from the consequences of hell!

Let's look at the facts about God's kingdom. Basically they are spelled out in His promises. We are forgiven; set free; heaven bound; in relationship with God; given the power of the Spirit; all things work for good for those who love and serve the Lord; given the opportunity to serve God himself, and many other wonderful opportunities. Remember the bottom line is to love "uncondition ally," but the rewards are beyond measure. By faith anything is possible.

I was told about a woman who cherished her granddaughter to such a degree that she bailed her out of any situation she ever had. As a result the young lady is now on drugs, has two DUI's and is looking at jail time. As I thought about all this, I realized I just never enabled my children, I always thought the consequences they would experience as children would keep them from future trouble, and in truth it did. But as I thought about it I realized it was more than that. I trusted that God would intercede for my children and protect them. It wasn't just nice words, I actually had the faith that He would. We throw a lot of spiritual words around, but we often don't believe them when put to the test. Now I knew my faith had certainly not come in a moment, but through many tests and trials. Now I'm sure many of my friends thought I was a bit loco at times, because I really did not worry and get concerned about much of anything. Often it was perceived as being cold hearted, but it's not that, I've had a lifetime of testing the Word of God, and He just never fails, so to live in the Kingdom of God is a complete trust that God's Word is true, and God will deliver the goods, no matter what it may be. Growing in Christ means to continue to know the Word of God, and put it to the test. Every time you get a positive result it makes you consider trusting God in another situation. You are then living in the Kingdom of God.

Now what are some of the attributes of a normal human being in the kingdom of this world or Satan's kingdom? We are programmed to concentrate on self. Me and mine, I want to live a good life, I want financial security, I want the perfect spouse, and the perfect kids, and the perfect house. We begin to focus on "me" very early in life. If I get a good education, it will open the door to the perfect everything. That's a high achiever but there are dozens of levels of what each person can spell out to get their impression of the perfect life. The interesting fact is when they get to the place they thought they wanted it's never enough, it doesn't fulfill them like we thought it would. Many people set a goal when they get married, to have a certain number of children, a nice house and most of the trimmings. They assumed it would take a life time, but when a couple are focused they reach that goal at 40 or so, and then it's like what now? There is an emptiness, they are not filled with the satisfaction of having achieved the goal of their dreams, and now an emptiness sets in. At this point they are vulnerable to whatever Satan puts before them, often it is another partner, or they focus on bigger and better things, anything to fill self! But peace and satisfaction seem to defy them. It is only temporary at best. Living in this world is a lifetime of disappointments. But living in the Kingdom of God leaves unending expectation of dreams we had never thought possible. There are possibilities that seem to unfold before you. When the body of Christ gets hold of Kingdom living they will change the world.

WHICH BIBLE SHOULD I USE

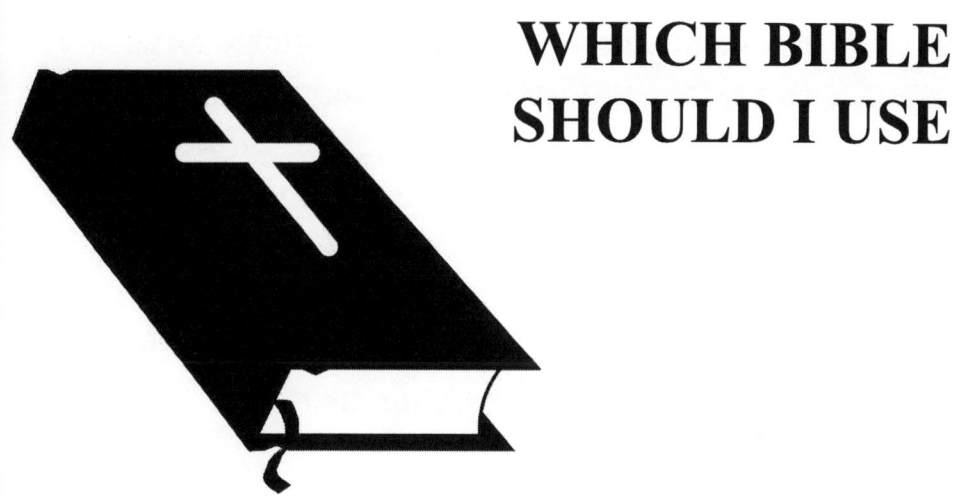

Some years ago a lady I knew had just finished her Pastoral training and was assigned to a church not far from me. Since I was almost through my training I decided to go to one of her Bible studies and see how she was handling things, maybe I could pick up a few points. She was rather an aggressive person, one of asked her what is the best Bible translation to use. She answered flat out (such and such a Bible) which is one of the newer more laid-back translations. There was no "in my opinion, or I prefer" she put it across as though this was the right one and the only one to use. Well it certainly was not the right one in my opinion. I went home rather frustrated, and said to the Lord, now I'm going to be in that position very soon, and I need to know how to answer that question, which is the right Bible to use? He soon answered me with this, "it's not what goes on the page that makes a difference, it's what comes off the page. Now I knew He was speaking of revelation knowledge. You know those moments when we've read this scripture a dozen times then all of the sudden it pops off the page and wakes you up to a complete new understanding of what is being said. So what He was telling me, is, that it doesn't matter which translation you use, He can give you a revelation anytime from any Bible. Now I have spent many years using one Bible or another, three to five years with one then another, but I have to honestly tell you I find I get much more Revelation knowledge using the New King James version than any other, that's just my experience.

Some of the newer ones printed after the turn of the century makes an effort to spell it out for you, and what you get is the writer's interpretation of the Word, personally I'm not crazy about that. Basically the writer gives you his opinion based on his maturity and that could be very limited.

When King James ordered the Bible to be translated into English in the 1700's, he called 47 Bible scholars together and they would divide up the work and each take a book and do their best to translate it. When finished they would join together and go over each other's translation until they were satisfied they had produced the best possible translation. All of them scrutinizing the work of each other, thereby getting the best possible interpretation of each book in the Bible. It is my understanding this format was followed for many years until I think in the 1990's when someone ordered a new Bible interpretation. It seems when they finished they did not call the scholars together to check each person's work. The scholars were very upset and vowed they would never do another translation. So which Bible should I use? I believe it's a good idea to start with one of the more simple translations for a period of time and then move to another. The "Good News Bible" was one I really enjoyed. It was only new testament, but it got me interested in the Bible, then I moved on to another translation. After several years of trying out different Bibles you will come to one that just seems to work for you. There doesn't seem to be a "right one" as many propose.

WHERE SHOULD I START READING THE BIBLE

As you begin to read the Bible, you are gaining some knowledge and getting a feel for the life and times of those days. It's best to start in the new Testament, you begin to understand who Jesus is and what all he did in those days. It is a good idea, if you can grasp the fact that what He did in those days never fails to be true for us today.

You will find the first four Gospel's, Matthew, Mark, Luke and John to be the same story from four different men's perspectives, also they have different audiences and try to make a point their audience would appreciate. The book of Acts tell how the Church began with the coming of the Holy Spirit, followed by letters different men wrote to help the new church grow, then of course Revelation is the promise of things to come. That's certainly a quick overview of the New Testament, but should give you a basic understanding to help you get started.

Once your comfortable with the New Testament then go to Genesis. Genesis covers a lot of material, some is difficult to understand, but keep going. Genesis lays out the beginnings of time on earth and the format of how God set up our foundation. It begins by laying out the plan God has for the future redemption of fallen man. His first order is to find a man he can have a relationship with and to trust, and one that will trust Him. He found that man in Abraham, and several generations later he eventually provided a family of twelve children God would train through a series of events to become His children, His heirs.

Much of the Bible deals with those families and the many times they strayed from God's teachings and the results of their waywardness. Best of all it gives many prophecies of future events that give us hope for tomorrow. We learn how God deals with us still today and the hope we can have because of the many stories revealed in the word. It is a book of hope and of promise. It is a Book that causes us to believe there is a heaven and a wonderful promise of life in the hereafter. In this book we learn that Jesus Christ took all our sins to the cross, and we can have a new life in Him just by accepting Jesus Christ as our Personal Savior, we can enter life everlasting.

WHAT'S THE DEAL WITH SATAN

Many people ask me is Satan real, does he have an influence in our life, does he have power?

Well its always best to see what the Word of God says. Now it is interesting, most of the information we have about Satan is from Jesus himself. Let's see what Jesus has to say about Satan.

The first encounter we have is when Jesus was baptized and went into the desert and fasted for forty days. Satan tempted Jesus from several different angles, but last he tempts him with the opportunity to rule all the kingdom's in the world. Jesus refuses the opportunity and says "it is written ye shall not tempt the Lord your God."

:   Next we see in Mark 4:15 the scripture about the sower and the seeds. "the sower sows the Word," "and these are the ones by the wayside where the Word is sown." (This would refer to those outside a church environment,) and when they hear, Satan comes immediately and takes away the Word that was sown in their hearts.

:   Next in Luke 13:16 Jesus has healed a woman and the scribes are complaining it was done on the sabbath, but Jesus replies, "so ought this woman, daughter of Abraham whom Satan has bound for eighteen years be loosed from her infirmities?

:   John 5:44 tells of Jesus speaking to the devil or possibly one of his spirits, and says you are of your father the devil, and the desires of your father you want to do, he was a murderer from the beginning, and does not stand in the truth, there is no truth in him, he is a liar and the father of it!

:   Next we see in Matthew 4:6 where Jesus is talking of the last days and says of the separation of mankind, on the right hand they will go to such and such a place, but He will say to those on the left hand, "depart from me you cursed into the everlasting fire prepared for the devil and his angels."

:   John 13:2, (the last Supper) the supper ended and the devil put it in the heart of Judas to betray him.

:   Mark 3:27, Jesus is telling the people "Satan cannot enter a strong man's house and plunder his goods unless he has bound the strong man first, then he can plunder his house."

(in these next few scriptures Jesus is talking of the last days)

:   John 12:31 Now judgment has come and the ruler of this world will be cast out.

:   John 16: 11, the ruler of this world is judged.

:   Matthew 25:41 two women will be grinding at the mill and one will be taken and the other left.

:   Romans 16:20, and the God of peace will crush Satan

:   In 1Peter 5:8 it say's , "be sober, be vigilant, because your adversary the devil walks about like a roaring lion, seeking whom he can devour.

:   2Cor 11:14 "No wonder! for Satan himself transforms himself into an angel of light.

:   2 Cor 2:11 (they are talking of the need to forgive,) and says "lest Satan should take advantage of us, for we are not ignorant of his devices."

Now I believe scripture says it all, Jesus acknowledged him as a real entity, so did his disciples who followed him, the question for us becomes well how!

Let's detail what Satan is accused of in these scriptures.

First, he tempts Jesus; second he takes away the Word sown in a person's heart; he creates dissension when Jesus heals a woman; he is a liar and the father of lies; then he puts evil in Judas heart to betray Jesus; next he binds the strong man to plunder the man's house; then he is an adversary seeking whom he can devour; last, he can transform himself into an angel of light; Now this is just some of the ways the Bible teaches about the ways of Satan.

Let's look at today's world and see the ways Satan has brought mankind under his influence. The obvious ones are drugs; alcohol; pornography; Cigarettes; obsessions with money, looks, dress, sex, possession's, relationships, even being opinionated . Now I'm probably missing many of them but you get the idea. Let's take being opinionated, you say oh that's just a trait that runs in the family, yea--really, well so does alcohol, drugs, obsession's with money, looks and dress. You see once a trait becomes an obsession your hooked, once your hooked you are no longer in control, oh I can quit if I really wanted to! How do you suppose you developed that trait. How far back does it run in your family? ------------ Satan has bound the strong man, at least one of the household, or the weakest personality, gets them hooked on anything, and generations later, the family is still fighting the battle. Most hooked people are blind to being hooked. Most people with strong obsessions, regardless of what that obsession is, will not confess their hooked. When they are addicted to anything, they are blind to it as well as family responsibilities because they are focused on their obsession. Their compulsion comes before responsibility. When your hooked, your blinded, and if your a parent, you will more than likely fall very short because you've got other things on your mind. Let's liken you to a big apple pie. As a whole pie the inside is protected by the crust, and good, but you take a bite out of the pie and it is exposed. When you have obsessive traits, your whole family is exposed and the enemy can come in and make havoc of your life. Maybe not in this generation, but down the line it will become evident. That's OK, Satan's got lots of time.

You know how young people are tempted to smoke or drink, or today smoke pot or take drugs. Well who do you think is behind that? Because once he gets one person hooked on something, he's got access to the whole family or future family. Once a person is obsessed, or hooked, or addicted it affects the whole family. You all know that. Is Satan real, yes, does he have influence yes, does he have power, yes, do we have power to stop him **yes!**

I used to say to the men in my drug addiction class, why do you think Satan choose to destroy your life? Then I tell them because you have such potential He knew you would be a threat to his kingdom. So do not let Satan blind your eyes to the truth. The Word of God clearly shows us that Satan is a real threat to the human race. Now let us understand that obsession leads to possession. In obsessive behavior, you feel compelled, drawn to, or anxious, you often say I've got to get rid of this habit, or this habit is killing, me but you still keep giving in to it. Now there are those who have the internal fortitude to come against it and overcome it. There are many who can advise you as to what steps to take to overcome this problem. Some say if you quit something for nineteen days it will go away, others say 27 days, personally I was hooked on a certain brand of soda pop and neither worked, I also will tell you as many of you know, you may quit for even a year, but the minute your guard is down, the opportunity will be presented to you and you say, oh why not, and what happens, your back. Obsession means your losing control, possession means you've lost control. Satan now has you under his control.

Now what hope do we have? In biblical days Jesus and his disciples had the power to cast out the demon, I'm sure you have read many of those examples. Now today, because of poor teaching most churches do not understand they are supposed to have that kind of power, the theologians or the power preachers have convinced you it only happened in Biblical days, however there are still some churches that believe in deliverance even though they are few and far between. There are many who are going through the motions for deliverance, but fail. One church I went to did deliverance ministry. I worked with some of the "deliverance ministers." How-ever it was clear they had learned all of the many steps to say, "do you renounce this or that," they go through a long page of questions, even some of them have memorized the whole page, but lacked the two things needed for deliverance which is discernment and a Holy life. I did not see one person delivered of anything. It takes a sold-out person to do deliverance, and to be honest, only a hand-full of people have that kind of relationship with God, and are mature enough to be effective, such as Benny Hinn, and the like. However, we are not without hope.

I read a story many years ago of a common housewife who had a neighbor whose son was paralyzed or something of that nature....serious stuff. God gave her a heart for the boy, but she didn't know what to do. God told her to fast and pray, after a long period of fasting and praying, she felt compelled to go and pray over him and he was totally set free. Now I'm going to share my under standing how this works, it's not the guidebook for deliverance, but just my understanding and for me it works. First as you will see in the above story, God gave her a heart for the boy. I'm sure you have had the experience when God has laid someone on your heart and you were just compelled to do something, particularly pray. Well that's because God is directing you and He has a plan for that person. Sometimes prayer is all you need. But not just a whisper of prayer, but hours of prayer over a period of time. Now he may call you to fast and pray. Be specific and disciplined. A set time for this and set time for that. You have been called to deliver someone from their situation. You are now called to be a minister of God, take it serious. Let's say you take one hour a week for prayer and a twenty-four hour fast. You do that for several weeks for this person and there may come a time when he will be delivered either with you or without you. What I mean is, God may deliver him just out of the blue, or he may call you to go pray over him. You will know what to do and when. It may take a year, or three months, whatever, God want's to use you. Let your prayer be, God, if I can be of help to someone let me know.

When I went after my 53 year old husbands soul, I saw a clock in my mind's eye, and it showed ten minutes after the hour. I didn't understand it at first, but what I did understand was this fervent compulsion to pray and fast for my husband. It would be there about a month, or even less, and then leave. Then it would come back and I could see the clock had moved ahead ten more minutes. Again I was compulsive to pray feverishly for a period of time and then it left me. Later once again it would return and I felt guilty for not keeping up my prayer, but it would just leave me. I continued to go through this over and over, and every time the clock would have moved ahead ten minutes. Then one day I saw it and it was twelve o'clock. On Sunday morning my husband said to me, you are so faithful in going to church and taking the boys, yet I know you are as tired as I am, as we had been out the night before. He said if you got my suit cleaned I would go with you. I got it cleaned and the next Sunday he said, if you would have gotten my suit cleaned I would go with you, I said I did get it cleaned, and he went. That was the beginning of my husband's road to salvation. I call it my ten to twelve theory. It took me about a year, and that was for salvation.

In my opinion there is a timing to these things. It's not to say that, if on your own you do a disciplined fast and prayer, God would not hear you, because we know he would. But listen to God and be sensitive to his voice.

Now I can assure you if your dealing with possession, it will take fasting and prayer, obsession maybe not. However, if you can get someone to be committed with you, you can more than likely shorten the time. Right now I have two people fasting with me for a thirty-six hour fast ever Monday, this will be the first time I've had the privilege of others joining me for a deliverance for someone on drugs. Just think, if he says where two or three are gathered together in my name and agree in prayer they shall have it.

Personally, I am not impressed with re-hab the medical world offers, as I've seen few permanent results, but some-times it's the only avenue available. Dealing with the demon takes fasting and the power of prayer, there is nothing in mankind that has the power to overcome possession. Only God has that power. It is a spiritual battle. Yes Satan is real!

In my opinion a person can seldom fast and pray for himself, because he is so obsessed with his problem, so what I tell those who feel called to help someone, is to help the person to build themselves up in the Word. Help them to find books with testimonies, get them into church where they are hearing the Word, if they are really ready to be set free, they will follow your instructions, then you do your thing. I know this is long and drawn out, but I pray that someone may get some help from it. I also strongly encourage you to get the support of a Pastor who believes in deliverance. Assemblies of God or Pentecostal churches, they may not be actually doing it, but they know about it and believe in it for the most part.

I want to share this story. Many years ago there was a woman on television being interviewed. I suspect it was a Christian program. The woman was a converted witch, and she shared how she would make every effort to get the neighbor kids into her house. I don't remember what all she did, but she did her best to influence the children into witchcraft. She said there was one neighbor whose children would definitely not respond to her. Once she was converted she went and visited with the mother of those children and as it turned out the mothers said she prayed for protection over her children every day. We really don't know the power of prayer, but it is encouraging to hear the testimony of those prayer warriors.

IF THERE IS ONLY ONE GOD WHY ARE THERE SO MANY CHURCHES

I always look to the Bible to see if there is some example to give us some insight as to answer the question. When we look at the early Church I believe they were of a survival mentality. There was so much opposition to these followers of Christ. At first they continued to worship in the Jewish synagogue and met privately as followers of Christ. Eventually they were not safe in the church and had to separate from the Jewish believers. In some areas they were persecuted and had to meet secretly. This battle went on for centuries and the church at times had to go underground. Leaders in the years 300 to 400 got together and created an order which eventually became the Catholic Church. There were many changes in the church for the next thirteen hundred years, but it continued to stay Catholic.

After 1517 the Roman Catholic church was losing its moral and political authority in some parts of Europe. Martin Luther a Catholic Priest upset the applecart with his "salvation by grace through faith alone." message. He eventually broke with the Roman Catholic Church in 1521. With this new twist in theology what we know as the Lutheran Church got it's start. He was encouraging church decision-making based solely on Bible study instead of tradition and canon law. He also opened the door for the use of the German language, instead of Latin.

Around the same year a Priest called Zwingli from Switzerland, was pushing reform. From his perspective the church was a community of Christians, voluntarily committed to imitating Christ to the world and to each other. This opened the door for the Amish and Mennonite Brethren to have their own worship service or "Church." The biggest battle had to do with deleting government control which was big in the Catholic Church. Baptism was another stumbling block, as well as salvation by grace through faith. The Catholics had a series of Sacraments they expected their followers to obey that would get them into heaven. Now these were focused on the Word of God and I'm sure their process was just as effective as the Protestant's. Now I might add just recently the Catholic Church has agreed with the Protestant faith that Salvation is by grace through faith.

Through the years other men started churches, John

Wesley founded the Methodist, then the Baptists and so on. This gives you an idea how we came to have so many denominations. To be honest there is very little difference between any of them, the exception based on their stand on baptism and communion.

When we study the Word we find the 'letters" in the New Testament, Romans, Corinthians, Peter, Jude and so on, these letters were written for specific needs, addressing problems each particular community was having in those days. They may be letters of encouragement, due to so much persecution. The letters were passed from church to church. However, in all these letters we do not find any particular structure advised for a church to follow, thereby leaving each congregation to design it's own. Through the years most have settled into pretty much the same structure. Opening praise, announcements, prayer requests, sermons and ending with praise. In some of the early churches you could not attend their service until there was definite evidence of your salva tion. I personally wish we would go back to that. I believe the church is meant to build up the body of Christ, encourage, teach and help to meet the needs of the parishioners, then reach out to the community. Unfortunately the saved are setting beside the unsaved, many who work their way up to positions in the church and have a say as to the direction of the church. Is it any wonder our churches have so much discord! Is it any wonder why so many of the churches want to do things the way the world does?

As I bring this to a close you can see the Bible does not define the structure of the church, He has left it up to man to form a church that will glorify, teach, encourage the body of Christ to grow in the likeness of Jesus Christ. We have had some excellent examples of Godly men who did their best to keep us on the right track. It is the responsibility of each parishioner to help keep it that way.

HOW CAN I KNOW WHAT CHURCH TO ATTEND

I have found churches have many faces, so to answer that question you need to answer this question, why do you want to go to church, what are you looking for. If you are new in the community you may want a church to help you get to know the people around you, basically for social interaction and to get involved. If your trapped in some form of addiction, you may want to attend for their support, your there because you need the body of Christ to help you through this challenge.

Then there are those who have had a recent spiritual encounter, and may want a church known for deep teaching, so they may grow. Also they may understand there is more to "church" than a social gathering of like-minded people and want to explore on a deeper level. We also have people who are reasonably mature who want to be in a place where they can serve God and use their gifts. Some may want a church where their children can be involved. And lastly there are those who have been touched by the Holy Spirit and want a service where they can express the fulness of their gifts such as tongues, prophecy and the like. Now once you've answered that question lets go on.

If your Catholic or Lutheran you know where you will be attending. Now these churches as well as the Baptists have different rites. Which means somewhere along the way someone disagreed with the leadership and broke off and started their own church, they kept the same original name but have just a different slant on things. So the point is, churches have different structures and it is a good idea to take an introduction class and find out just what that church is all about. Just because it's friendly does not mean it will line up with your theology.

I might add there is the Mormon, the Latter Day Saints, and the Jehova Witness that are not based on the Christian understanding of salvation as we do. They very nice people but who the Christian denomination believes are misled. Remember Satan comes as an angel of light to deceive who he might and if you are looking for a church for the first time you are a prime target. Now let me give you a general idea of the focus on some of the main denominations.

Methodist: Believers in salvation through faith, infant or adult baptism, community minded, focused more on personal maturity, in the last ten years have moved pretty far to the left, however there is a small percentage who have had some revival and are doing an excellent job. They are very serious about evangelism in other countries.

Baptist, many branches, believe in salvation through faith, Do not believe in infant baptism, very strong in recruiting and bringing others into the fold, Community minded.

Holiness churches, lots of do's and don't, but make an effort to live the gospel. More focused on personal holiness.

Nazarene churches seem to have cut themselves off from the general public social world, really focus on Godly lifestyle, quite a few do's and don't, but develop into real Godly people.

Lutheran are of course Protestant, after all they started the movement, but have kept up more stringent methods of worship. Very serious about personal holiness, Do not appear to be outgoing or evangelistic, yet in their silent way they may be. I would say they tend to be very private about their walk with God.

Assembly of God and Pentecostal churches are open to the gifts of the Holy Spirit, such as tongues, deliverance, and prophecy, focused on holiness.

Today's churches are going through a serious transition, and because of it non-denominational churches have sprung up everywhere. I welcome it as the old line protestant churches have lost their influence in society. Each of these churches have their own focus, but many are really working on local social action. They are feeding the Word to masses of people without any strings at tached. Some open with high praise and often longer then I personally like, but it is good to see their enthusiasm. They will make their mark on society at a time when we really need it. I personally would encourage you to shop around and see if any of these churches might fulfill your needs.

Don't be afraid to change churches, sometimes we outgrow churches and need to move on to continue growing spiritually. Others are happy to grow where their planted. Often you will find that if you have gifts, such as teacher or the gifts to minister to others you may need to go where they are open to your gifts.

Last, remember Pastors have their limits, and each

have their gifts, some are extremely good at community involvement, some good at teaching and others at ministering to the body of Christ. Some do a fantastic job of preaching and are extremely good on the alter, but you don't have to be all that spiritual to be a good preacher. Those who are hungry for God often outgrow their preacher and would do themselves a favor by finding another church, no matter how nice the Preacher is. For me the bottom line is to grow spiritually, not to just settle in a comfortable religious setting, where I'm OK I know I'm going to heaven and I don't need to continue to seek more of God. The call to Christianity is to follow Christ and become like him. That takes consecrated effort.

THE BAPTISM OF THE HOLY SPIRIT

Many people have heard of the baptism of the Holy Spirit and want to know more about it. There is much controversy over the subject. There are those who have been "filled with the Holy spirit," and claim you must experience it much like they did or you haven't got it. There are those who say it only happened at Pentecost, as in the Acts of the apostles, and does not happen today. I will give you my two cents worth of information, and you can make up your own mind.

Let's first look at what happened in the Act's account. Acts 2: Many of the believers were praying together, suddenly a sound came from heaven as a rushing mighty wind and it filled the whole house. Then there appeared to them divided tongues, as of fire, and one sat on each of them, and they were all filled with the Holy Spirit and began to speak in other tongues as the spirit gave them utterance.

This is what it would appear, you could expect if you are filled with the Holy Spirit. It is the first example of His outpouring and why shouldn't we expect pretty much the same thing.

History validates these occurrences to have happened many times through the centuries. History also reveals they too experienced the same phenomenon as the first Apostles did. There can be no question as to it happening since Pentecost, anyone can look on the internet and see historical records of these occurrences. Several of the experiences during the 1800s are well documented. There are also many books that share the experiences of those happenings. In the early 1900's there was a large outpouring in California, of which the Pentecost church got its start, and I am quite sure also the Assemblies of God. In the late 1960's the Catholic church had an outpouring which spilled over to many of the other churches and lasted about 15-20 years. In late 1990's it happened in Toronto and was so widespread people came from all over the world to experience the outpouring. So is it real, absolutely! Have I experienced it? Absolutely!

How can I explain it? It is my opinion when our old world gets so bogged down and out of sorts, God in His mercy sends a revival to stir up the spirit in the church to revive us. Let's be honest, without the Holy spirit there is no church, we would be just another do-good organization. Save the whales or whatever.

So God sends revival now and then to stir up the Church and help to get it back on track. It is always controversial, because it's not what were used to. Anything that is new and not how it happened "to me" is subject to challenge. That's why we don't build our religion on what man says, but on what God says, and when it lines up with the Word we know were right with God, even if were not right with "those" in the church who challenge our experience.

Now what is the problem. It would appear when Godly people, who have been steadfast in the church for years see the new fire in some of the church members, and these members are actually speaking in tongues and are displaying some of the gifts, such as prophecy, they often go into denial. I mean it didn't happen to them. So they don't see how it could have happened to someone else, so it must not be real, and the argument begins. Newly filled people look on the older people as though they don't have the Holy Spirit because there are none of the gifts being displayed. Unfortunately it takes quite a long time, before the newly filled people come to realize people can be filled and overflowing with the Spirit without the gift of tongues and the like. Most of the gifts such is teacher, server, mercy, administrator are evident in the church body and quietly serving God in a variety of ways.

There is often the challenge, I've got more of the Holy Spirit then you do and people don't like that. We might be reminded that love is the measuring line, not a prophetic message, or outburst of tongues.

So if your one of those who were blessed with an in-filling of the Holy Spirit, don't be to judgmental on those who have not had the privilege of sharing your experience, nobody ever said Abraham spoke in tongues. Remember the bottom line is always to become servants, and to love one another.

Now here are some questions so often asked. Why do some receive visible evidence of it others do not. The people it happened to in 1970 that I am familiar with, were very hungry for more of God. It seemed anyone I shared it with, wanted it and received it, we ended up with a large group, but those main friends were already active in the church. Those outside that circle were not interested. It spread like wildfire in the churches, and went from church to church.

Did they all speak in tongues? There were several hundred people in the groups I was associated with and most spoke in tongues, however, some did not. I don't know why.

How did you know they were spirit filled if they did not speak in tongues? To be honest you never knew. However, I know I was filled with the Spirit for several months before I spoke in tongues, and there were several others who did not get the gift of tongues right away. I will say I begged, and pleaded with God for the tongues, because at the time I thought you didn't have it unless you had the gift of tongues, then the Lord revealed to me that I had been filled months before. I told God you've got to give it to me, because your Word says! ask and it will be given unto you, so you gotta give it to me. What I do with it after is another thing, but your Word says! ...Oh I was bold, but I stood on the word. I won't say that's right or wrong, just that's what I did to get the gift of tongues, but I was already filled with the Spirit many months previous.

Being Spirit filled is what I liken to getting high on drugs, you get a super dose of the love of God and it's the only things you care about. Now I can't say that is everyone's experience, but it was mine. I liken it to a road going up a mountain, your driving and as you climb you gotta shift down, then as it gets steeper you gotta shift down some more and so on, but if you are Spirit filled your in overdrive, bottom line you both get to the top. Now when people get saved they have been touched with the Holy Spirit, you can't have God without the Spirit. It just seems now and then God dumps an overdose on the church.

Since the resurrection of Christ, the Spirit of God has been drawing men into the salvation experience, there would be no Church if it were not for the move of the Spirit, salvation is a spiritual movement with or without tongues. Some people don't get them, because there is a certain reserve in them and they are uncomfortable about it. I've known many Godly people that I wish I could be as beautiful as they are that don't speak in tongues. They may often have many of the gifts other than the gift of tongues.

The only problem I have about it is that I know the value of praying in the Spirit or tongues, and personally I wish all prayed in the Spirit, but that's God's job not mine, and as long as I am faithful to His calling that's all I've got to worry about. I will say this, those who did not receive the gift of tongues when filled with the Spirit seemed to have to work hard to get the tongues. One of my friends spent a year before she got them, another friend spent close to a year. Why? I have no idea.

Also it seems when the move of the Spirit is over it doesn't happen for a period of time. It's like He dumps it on a certain spot, and those nearby receive it and it spreads wonderfully for a period of time, then dies out. I have said for years those who got it in the 1960-90's, he is cleansing and teaching so when the next movement comes He will have teachers and prophets available to minister to those He will be calling in the next wave.

Derick Prince and others have prophesied there would be another great movement and it would happen in the South/East part of North Carolina. Seeing is believing, let's hope he's right.

Now tongues seems to be the only controversial portion of the Holy Spirit, but there are other gifts. In Corinthians and Roman's the Word likens it to a human body with different parts, but all work together for the same good. They are listed as prophesy; teaching; exhortation; giving; administration, serving and mercy, all are to build up the body of Christ. Some consider the ministry of prophesy, :as prophet, one who proclaims the Word. :Teacher is explaining the word, :Exhortation is like a counselor, :administration, one who sizes up a situation and be put in charge, :serving are those who are always convicted to help people in anyway possible, :giving is one who is usually generous in giving and :mercy are those who have unending compassion for those who are being challenged. The server feel they are just more tuned in to the needy, when in fact God has blessed them with a heart for helping those in need. Let us understand that God has touched the heart of all those to minister out of their gift.

Let me just share a few insights; a server is the women who do the funeral dinners, or the men who fix the roofs of the old ladies houses, they are compassionate and kind, they believe everybody should be helping when in truth God has gifted them in that capacity. But it seems they will work till they drop, they serve the people in the church as well as in the community.

The Prophet is not necessarily to prophesy future events, but a standard bearer, to keep the body focused on the direction a church should be headed in from a spiritual standpoint.

The Exhorter is one who sees a problem and offers help in a step by step process, not just proclaiming what to do about this problem, but sees things in stages, and can help advise those in need.

The Administrator, is one who is conscious of the gifts of people around them and can help direct the right people to fulfill the needs of the body of Christ. They are not to do the work, but put the right person in the right place.

The Teacher is one who always wants things done in a step by step process. You can't do step three until you've done step one and two. It is easy to know if your a teacher not only because you want to share the Word but because any event where there is a speaker, they will be the one asking questions, "like, I don't dis-believe what you say, but how did you come by that?"

Giving is often associated with people who are able

to make big bucks, and often share it privately. The givers in my church would come to me and hand me money and say, the Brown kids need shoes, you go and buy them but don't tell where the money came from.

The easiest way to describe the gift of mercy is that they will give an alcoholic his last bottle, because they can't bear to see the person in agony. They are full of love and compassion.

Now that is just a quick overview of the fulness of the Holy Spirit. As you know these gifts are evident in most churches even if they are not identified as gifts of the Spirit. People may not recognize they are operating out of a gift that God gave them, they just think they have a heart for teaching or whatever. However, if you can identify your gift, then you can enhance it. Also when you know your gift, then you can also see the gifts in others. By recognizing these gifts, you can encourage people to focus on doing just what they are gifted for, and also make room for that person to exercise their gift. I will add this, often a person with the gift of administration does not understand they are not to do the work, they are to recognize the gifts of others and present them with the work at hand. Administrators often get involved in doing the work and interfere with those gifted for the job.

When I was a young woman I had a friend who was Johnny on the spot, her name was Sandra. If someone were sick, she would take a casserole over, if someone needed a ride some where she would take them, I believe she must have made a million cookies and gave them away, not to speak of the basket of flowers she grew to give away, and then there was her crocheting and of course she baked homemade bread and gave it away. Well before I became reasonable mature in Christ, I too had the desire to take a pie to a hurting family, but never seemed to get to it. Oh I had good intentions, but no follow-through. My friend had the gift of serving, she was motivated to follow through with a natural drive to meet the needs of those who had a need. I know I believed we should always be a good Christian which meant to do good things for people, but I did not have the gift of serving. When I realized I had the gift of teaching, it removed my guilt for not serving, and I involved myself in sharing the Word to the best of my ability. God designed the church for His children to have this variety of gifts to meet all the needs of the body of Christ, and though we must always be motivated to love one another, we will see we are gifted in some specific way.

Now we have talked about the gifts of the Spirit, and personally I have stuck to the teachings of Oral Roberts, his teaching was excellent and made sense. Others have different versions, but very little difference between any of them. However, we have another aspect of the Spiritual outpouring and it has to do with the manifestations of the Spirit. These are manifestations of healing; word of wisdom; understanding; word of knowledge; discernment; working of miracles; faith; healings; and prophecy. Now do not confuse these with the gifts, the gifts are a permanent part of who you are. You are motivated to teach, or feed the poor, serve the people of God in however you are gifted. But a manifestation happens in the spur of the moment. You may be talking with someone and all the sudden you share an insight, it might be some wisdom, or a word of knowledge or discernment. When you share the person is usually quite blown away, and to be honest, you are too. You think where did that come from. These gifts just manifest through anyone at anytime. But they are not something you can count on permanently. You may all the sudden feel the call to pray over a person and they get healed. I think when God wants something done he uses whoever is there. But learn to be sensitive to these callings and open to them. God want's to enhance His presence and is always looking for a few good men.

Many years ago I went to a Holy Spirit Convention and one of the speakers was a young man who was studying to be a Priest. I felt very led to talk with him after the service and found him in the back of the church. In taking to him, I said I feel God is calling him to leave the Priesthood and pursue something else. Now I don't know how I worded it, but he was absolutely shocked, and said thank you for sharing that because that is exactly the problem he was facing, and it confirmed his suspicion's. Now I'll be honest, I was very new in the spirit and have no idea how I phrased it, but I wouldn't be near so bold today. But it was a Word of knowledge for him, and the Spirit compelled me to bring it up to him.

These manifestations occur on a moment's notice, and you may have experienced it yourself. Now there is much more to share about this Holy Spirit business, but the above gives you some idea about it all. I encourage you to seek all you can about God, because all of it brings joy to the one who receives, regardless of the degree of the move of God.

WHAT ABOUT TV EVANGELISTS

The real questions is can we trust them, are they on the up and up? Let me address this from a few different perspectives. First there are people who really run them down, and most definitely would not listen to them. Why would that be?

In the early twenties and through the fifties a good share of our population had at least some sort of religious training. Maybe not a lot but at least enough to know the basics. How-ever there was a great falling away following those years, and what was learned as a child is the finality of their understanding of religion. Therefor most people are stuck in the same theology they learned as a child and are adamant, they got it all. Masses of people don't go to church any more but when religion comes up they are ridged in in their beliefs. They are stuck in Daniel and the lion's den, Joseph with his coat of many colors, Shadrach, Mesach and Abed-Nego, never learning the lesson behind the story, they just know the story. The truth is, the story continues to unfold. You might look at it like this, if you graduated from high school, you could now say, I never have to learn another thing in life, I got it all. That is the attitude of those who don't go to church, but have much to say about it.

We are dealing with a new wave of spiritually, and this new wave is a threat to those who will use any excuse to keep from a relationship with God.

Fortunately, God has provided an alternative. He made it clear that the gospel was to be heard around the world so he has presented us with those who have a heart to share the word through the media.

I think TV evangelists fill a great need for all of us. It enhances those who are hungry for God, it opens doors for those who just happened to listen to one of them and their message may draw them back into the fold.

Many years ago Oral Roberts was on TV and I truly disliked him, but one day I ended up hearing one of his messages and actually liked it. I continued listening to him and became a believer in his ministry, even to the point of going to Tulsa for a long weekend retreat. What happened? The truth is I was now ready for his message, I began to learn about tithing and all that goes with it.

Learning to tithe in my estimation opens the door to a deeper level of spirituality. You begin to see God on a more personal level. However, once I consumed his message, I lost interest, but that was after many years of following him. Then I went on to Schuller, who didn't have much to offer as far as I was concerned, however once he caught my attention I realized his message was learn to love yourself, and all that goes with it. As I considered the evangelists I thought each of these men seem to have one basic message, Billy Graham has one message -salvation. Oral Roberts, the blessings of being obedient in your finances, Schuller love of who you are, Stanley walk the Word.

As you look at the men and woman evangelists today, each has a certain point they drive home. They can cover those messages from Genesis to Revelation, but they still only have one point. Olstean has one message, take the challenges in life and find God in it. He's working to build up the body of Christ piece by piece. Stanley is another great teacher.

It's good to look at the message and decipher the main point of their message. Some have messages of Revelation and the return of Christ. I honestly believe most of them are on the up and up. God continues to open our eyes to new revelation when we are ready for it, but when were not we tend to be critical. Now it takes money to do TV broadcasting, and for them to ask for help is not out of line, but when it is overdone you will probably sense it. But don't throw the baby out with the wash. If we are not ready for a certain message we may be turned off by them. I really disliked Oral Roberts for years, but I learned more from him than any other preacher, his teachings are still the basis of much of what I teach. Realize those evangelists are probably meeting the needs of many.

I think it is great that God has laid it on the hearts of evangelists to press a point to help the body of Christ grow. Think of the elderly or handicapped who can't get out, isn't it neat for God to find ways of getting His message out across the nations. God said to take the message to the world.

Many years ago I read some of Benny Hinn's books and was sold on him, a new voice enlarging the message. I had an opportunity to see him in Florida. It was Good Friday and the place was packed. Even though I was already confident in him, I went in with much reserve. I thought I'm not going to get sucked into something I'm not comfortable with, so I sat in the very back row, I mean the row of chairs against the back wall so I could get out fast if needed. It was so dumb, but I wanted to observe very closely. Now I was not impressed with the choir, then he came out and I was struck by the fact he was such a small man, and all I did was focus on the negative. By the end of the service, I was still scrutinizing his every move. At last he invited everyone to come forward. Now there were thousands there and I was flat out in the back. I thought well I came here to see him so I might better go forward, knowing I would not get very close. As I began to walk forward, there was a sign behind the choir that said, "if you will believe you will see the glory of God." I thought what is the matter with me, I believed in him before I came, so I took my eyes off the negative and focused on the sign. I repeated it over and over to myself. Then all the sudden, it was like a rock hit me and knocked me over and I hit the floor with a bang. I mean I didn't crumble to the floor but went straight back and since there was no one behind me, I hit the floor flat out. I slowly pulled myself up and slipped into a pew and hung on to the pew to keep myself upright. I eventually left and for two weeks the Spirit of God was so strong on me I could hardly talk. Needless to say I nearly missed a blessing because I was so focused on the negative. So I encourage you to be open, and try not to focus on the things you don't like, but listen to the message, God may have a real surprise for you. If you truly have a problem with the theology of the speaker, then do some checking in the Word, maybe he has a point God want's you to pick up.

IS THE DEVIL REAL

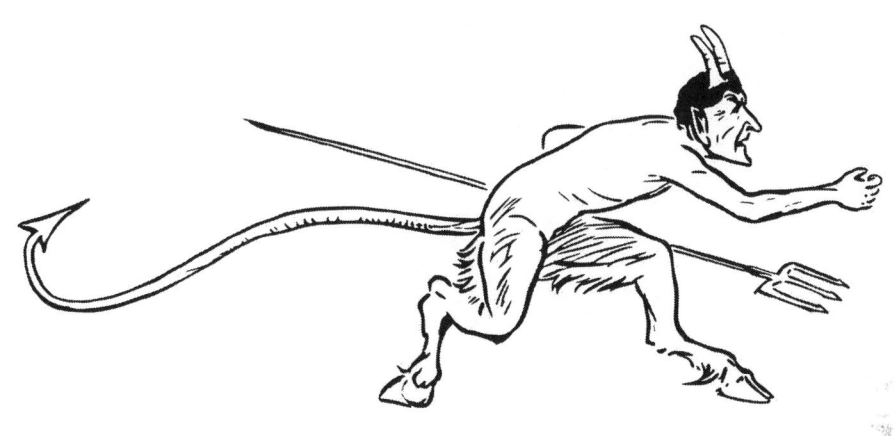

I just want to make a few comments about our belief or non-belief in the Devil. I know I covered it to some extent before. But If your going to be a Christian then it is important to understand that Satan is a real entity. His mode of operation is to make you believe he is not. Satan influenced Eve with a lie and a deception. "Oh" the apple will make you wise, and there was no mention of consequences. We often laugh a little when we say "oh the devil made me do it," "ha-ha" the truth of it is, it's possible the devil did influence you to do it. The greatest deception he has managed to do is to convince us he is not real.

THE REALITY OF RELIGION

I often think our rendition of religion is somewhat like Santa Claus. We are led to believe there is this man dressed in a red outfit whose belly is like a bowlful of jelly. He comes once a year and brings us the list of toys from our want list, of which we wrote to him about. He rides through the air from the north pole in a sleigh, being pulled by twelve reindeer whose leader is the smallest of them all, and who has a nose that glows in the dark. He makes every house in one night, lands on the roof and slides down the chimney leaving the toys, eating the cookie we left him, and then scoots back up the chimney without ever getting dirty, and on to the next house. The wide array of toys he delivers are made by strange looking little elves that live in the North Pole.

Somewhere between five and eight we learn this is not really true. Now for a few there may be a meltdown, but for the most part the children have already had a few doubts, and handle it just fine. Why? Because somewhere along the way they have come to realize reindeer do not fly, an extremely fat man could not possibly get down the chimney, especially if we don't have a fireplace, let alone zoom back up. They have come to realize the world is a pretty big place and no one could possibly make It to every home in the world in one night, and then the elves? After living in the real world, they have come to a realistic understanding due to the simple facts of life along the road their eyes have been opened to.

Unfortunately, I think religion goes through a similar scenario. We learn in Sunday school as children how an unusual small boy named David killed a giant named Goliath with a sling-shot, how the three men in the fire didn't burn no matter how hot the fire got, how the den of lions did not eat up Daniel even though they were so hungry they ate the bad men before they hit the ground. We learn how thousands of people were led through the wilderness for forty years and got water out of a rock. We learn how the iron axe head floated, and Elijah when he died rose from the ground and was taken up by a chariot into the heavens. Then of course, Jesus walked on water, rose the dead, healed the sick, fasted forty days and made the blind to see.

Now it's not difficult to let go of Santa, because I have no need of him once I understand my parents carry on the role. Actually, I probably have a better chance with them anyway. He is not an identity I am going to need in my tomorrow, but Jesus is a different story. I associate Jesus with going to heaven. If I believe in Him then I should alter my life and make an effort to be obedient to his teachings. But since all I have are these quite extraordinary tales I learned in Sunday School, it is quite easy to question them. And then if I go to college it is a cinch for the college professors to convince me they are not that much different than the Santa hoax. I have not seen anything of the supernatural in my years of Sunday School that would convince me to alter the direction I choose to follow for my life. Also, if these supernatural experiences are an established standard for religion, I'm not sure they line up with the way I want to live my life, so it is easier to call them a hoax.

Now we have a similar situation with young adults who come back to church. Somewhere along the way, they have lost faith in the supernatural as an attainable entity for their Christian walk, though for the most part they still believe the stories. Now the establishment of Churches do not set the standard of holiness out of reach, which makes it comfortable for the average person to live in a complex world and still be a part of the body of Christ. **The church keeps the supernatural as a historical part of their history.** The standard for the church is now to be a social gathering of people who are of one mind and love the Lord. They make an effort to impact the world around them by doing good deeds.

Their basic theology is to accept Jesus Christ as their Savior, get baptized, and do their best to obey the ten commandments. The church has lowered the standard of religiosity to make it comfortable to be a part of the family of God. But what is the real truth, does the bible reveal what a real Christian is supposed to be like, or does it give us any hints as to what to expect if we have become Christians. Is there a change?

Now for the most part people have had a religious experience when they got born again, they can't explain it, but something definitely happened. Certainly they felt a level of love, and surely were set free, somehow they sensed they were forgiven. What does Jesus say about all this.

As I study the scriptures one thing becomes absolutely clear, the Kingdom of God the Bible speaks of and the world I live in are two separate places. Let's look at some scriptures. In Mark 1:15, it says the time is fulfilled and the Kingdom of God is at hand.

Matt. 3:2 Repent for the Kingdom of God is at hand. Ephesians 5:5 no sinner has any inheritance in the Kingdom of God. Colossians 1:13 He has delivered us from the power of darkness and translated us into the Kingdom of God. John 3:5, unless we are born of water and the spirit we cannot enter the Kingdom of God, what is born of flesh is flesh what is born of Spirit is Spirit.

I believe these great stories in the Old and New Testament were documented so that we could get an image of what a real relationship with God through Jesus and what we should be striving for. A spiritual life should be a supernatural life. We live a hum-drum life and it is only until we hit a wall we do then cry out "help me God." Yet scripture has already told us, Ask and ye shall receive. We are seeking God to intervene in a supernatural way to meet a need. Now if He answers, do you not realize it is a supernatural event. You prayed to an invisible God and got an answer. That is a supernatural event. Any response from God has to do with the supernatural. If it's supernatural, your dealing with the Kingdom of God. Look at these scriptures, "if two or three agree on earth concern ing anything they ask, it will be done in the midst of thee." " if you abide in me and My words abide in you, ask what you desire and it shall be done." "Whatsoever you ask the Father in my name it will be given you."

John 18:, "My kingdom is not of this world". When we accepted Jesus Christ as our savior, got baptized, we then entered a spiritual world, but we continue to live in Satan's world and only cry out for the supernatural world when were hurting. God wants us to live in His kingdom now, not wait until I die. The Word says, " all these things shall be added unto you," what, every promise in the Bible. "But seek first the Kingdom of God and His righteousness and all these things shall be added unto you, your life, what you eat, drink and in the workplace."

Now the key to this kingdom is faith and He wants for us to live in it daily, not just when we have a crisis. We begin with little things.

I get into the car, whisper a prayer, God let the blood of Jesus be over me, and the angels surround me, keep me safe, help me to be sensitive to traffic, and help me make wise decisions. When you've said that continuously you begin the believe it, you feel you are in a bubble and God's got your back. That little area is now kingdom living. I am going to the supermarket, and need a close parking space so I pray when I get going and when I get there He has one already for me. I've had people ride with me and say they can't believe how there is always a spot for me. I expect God to take care of me because he wants to take of me. Matt:6 He said no one can serve two masters; he cannot serve God and mammon, therefore I say to you, do not worry about your life, what you will eat or what you will drink, not about your body, what you will put on. Is not life more than food and body more than clothing. Look at the birds of the air, for they neither sow nor reap nor gather, into barns; yet your heavenly father feed them, Are you not of more value then they?

When you begin to exchange worldly values for spiritual values, you get set free. The Word says judge not that you not be judged. When you let go of your opinions of people and situations, which are of a judgmental nature you will not then be judged in your own shortcomings. This is Kingdom living. Each of these areas increase your faith, so that when you need a miracle you have the faith to expect one. As I grow in Christ my values change, it's not nearly as important to be the big shot in the company, it's not so important my child be the lead in the dancing class. There's such a freedom to let go of worldly values. I lean more and more on God and find I trust Him more and more. That's kingdom living, not my will but thine be done.

Were walking in the Kingdom if we have come to trust God in our health, job, children, finances, what we wear, where we live, and what we drive. Always remember God want more for you then your desires can comprehend. Each time we yield an area it builds our trust in His care, so that when we have the big one and desperately need a miracle our faith can carry us through.

THE SILENT WITNESS

Many years ago, I was in one of the most difficult times of my life. It was the darkest season I experienced since I became sold out for Christ. I was in such pain that all I wanted to do was run away, anything just to get away from the pain. I ended up going to my sisters 250 miles south. I had a meager amount of cash to hopefully carry me through until I got a job.

Now my sister was not a believer, she believed in it but it was not for her. She never gave you space to share the gospel in anyway. It was alright for you, but she didn't need it. Now she was a wonderful supportive sister and treated me so kind in my darkness. She would watch my son while I went out to look for jobs. She would make suggestions, but I would say oh God is going to open a door for me, and I would adamantly speak of my faith in this God who knows my circumstances and he will come through. Day after day of disappointment I professed His faithfulness. I thought this is a time when God can really come through to prove how faithful God is to His children. I'm sure he will work a miracle and she will want to become a Christian. The days became weeks, and no job. Though I continued to confess my faith in God to my sister, in the night I would have a good cry and let God know just what I thought of this let down. My money was almost gone and it was a challenge to keep a good face on. One day I finally got a simple job working in a large Doctor's office making very little money. Not much to say "see what my God did for me"! My sister continued to stand by me and eventually things worked out and I got on with my life. I was always a little disappointed that God did not reveal Himself is such a way as to make a difference to my sister, I mean He missed a wonderful opportunity, right! Years later I was talking to my mother about the whole thing and she said, Oh, didn't you know your sister shared with me that as far as she was concerned you were the greatest Christian she ever knew.

I learned a big lesson in that experience. I learned it is not how your challenge ended that speaks to the observer, but how you handled yourself while going through the challenge. I have seen this be true in many situations. I think this is also true of God. He knows how the story ends, but can you be faithful through the trial.

Remember He's looking for a few good men!

Now I'm sure you want to know how the story ended with my sister, did she come to know the Lord. To be honest I don't know. Through the years she shared how on two occasions someone shared with her in detail the gospel, she said, she was on the dock fishing for lobsters in Florida when a man shared for hours, and she would say, oh you would like to talk to my sister, but in the end she would say it's not for her. Another time she was in a donut shop and another man was sharing to the point they left the restaurant because they were taking up seats that were needed. She told me they talked for an hour leaning on her car, but she told him the same thing, oh you would love to talk to my sister, but in the end she would say it's not for me. I was with her for many months before she died, she was a good woman, helped a lot of people, but bottom line, I just don't know. She may have gotten saved as a child in Sunday School, she lived a good life that could be considered Christian. I'm so glad it's not my place to say who goes into heaven, because I think we may have a lot of surprises. But I sure hope I get to see my sister.

MY FAITHFUL FATHER

When I was in my early fifties I had gone through all the hoops to become a Pastor and was anxiously awaiting the day when the District Superintendent would call me and give me an assignment. In the mean-time I was about my usual daily life with my two teenagers, husband and Tom. Tom was a young man I had taken in from a homeless shelter. Now this was not an unusual thing for me as I had taken in strays for about twenty years, If I didn't bring someone home, then my husband did. We had a humungous house and plenty of room. Tom had been through a drug rehab place and was in hopes of getting on with his life. To be honest, he had more potential then most of the young men I took in. He picked up a simple job and was doing well.

My husband and I often took little jaunts to work on our genealogy studies for maybe two or three days at a time. Since Tom had proven himself to be pretty responsible young man we felt we could trust him to keep an eye on our two teenagers. We left Tom in charge with many instructions and left for our little outing.

We came back three days later and my husband's truck was not in the yard. Well the boys said, Tom took it the day we left and hasn't returned. Now Tom was from Detroit in the heart of the toughest section of the City. He was raised by his grandma. We called the police of which they flat out told me, lady, that truck will have been stripped within twenty-four hours after it was taken, so forget about getting it back. Now I can tell you my husband was raging, to say the least. But I always had faith, my God, who is all sufficient will supply all my need according to his riches in glory, in other words he won't leave me hanging. Now I had grandma's phone number of which I quickly made good use of. She was all upset, but told me she would check on a few things and call me right back. I sat practically on the phone and when it rang I practically yelled, what did you find out, I didn't say hi, hello or whatever. Then I heard on the phone this gentle voice of a man who said, it this Mary Spencer---well this is John Huhtala the District Superintendent. Oh no, of all the times you want to sound like you got it all together, and instead you sound like raving idiot. So he did his polite thing and gave me an appointment to meet with him. I tried to quickly explain what was up and why I answered the phone is such a manner.

Well I got the call from grandma and the she told me

Tom would be home in about an hour and I could talk to him. Well I got her address and instead of waiting for the call, my 15 year old son and I drove to the house in Detroit. We waited outside about a block from the house, but where I could see if Tom came home. When he came meandering in we pulled right in behind him and said, where's the truck. Well Tom being the nice guy he was supposed to be said, well- I ah -I sold it. But, he said the guy still has it because I've seen him driving it. Tom had sold it with a fake incorrect title. I said, take me to it. Well Tom said I can show you where it's at but he can't see me. So he got in the back of the van, slid down so he couldn't be seen and took us to the house of the guy who owned it. Then would you believe the guy pulled right up in front of the house and parked in the street.

Now we had driven around quite a bit before we actually found the house and in doing so I had seen a cop car some distance away. So I headed back to find the cop. Now I explained the story to him, but he was raving mad, woman what are you doing in this neighborhood, I can't do anything about your truck. But then he finally said, well take me to the street where the trucks at. All the time Tom's hid in the back of the van. We drive to the truck parked in the street and the cop makes a u turn and pulls up behind the truck, and orders me to pull up beside him. Is this your truck? You got a title to it, and so on. I said I saw the guy get out of the truck and he went into this house, indicating for us to go to the door. He said lady are you crazy, we ain't going up to that door, your in the most dangerous part of Detroit. But then the guy saw the cop's car out front he came out of the house. (ain't my God good) he said what's wrong officer, the cop said, you got a title for that truck? he said yes I do, and went and got it out of the truck. I looked at the title and showed the cop, that's not the right title, the year is wrong and so is the type of truck. The guy realized he'd bought a hot truck and stuck his head in the passenger side window and said you tell Tom if I ever see him he's dead meat. Tom's still hiding and shuttering in the back. The cop said OK lady get in the truck and get out of here.

Well that meant my 15 year old son had to drive my van and follow me out of this maze of blocks which went on for miles. Tom's in the van behind me and I'm in the truck weaving in and out of blocks trying to get out of the neighborhood, men on the street are whistling to the truck because they think the other guy is in it. I mean it was an experience I won't soon forget. We had to drive 75 miles back to Flint. Tom said take me with you. We got the truck back and I hid Tom in one of the second-floor bedrooms and went to the third floor where my husband and I slept. My husband was quite shocked we actually got the truck back, and then he started yelling about Tom and said don't you let him in this house again and on and on. Here Tom was in the bedroom just below him…..hmmm I'm walkin on pretty thin ice, but the next day I took Tom to Grand Rapids to another drug rehab and that's the end of the story and I lost track of Tom. It's probably better that way.

A few days later I went to meet with the District Superintendent and when I got there he asked me, what was all that about when I called you. So I told him the whole story, and a few years later, he told me it was because of my tenacity in how I handled the truck situation that got me the wonderful church I ended up with. He said if I can handle that kind of a situation then I could surely handle any church.

IN CLOSING

Now you might say what has this to do with a spiritual book that's intended for teaching? Well I thought about the story itself as a reflection of how God works in just every day life. Now this was not necessarily an everyday life experience, however God is all over it. My faith was real and reasonably solid. As I thought about it I wondered how did I become so confidant facing this situation; How did I find my way to this section of Detroit; I've never been there before in my life and certainly not at night. We had no GPS; how was I so sure I would get the truck back? As I look back I realize the one reason why I could go through this experience was because of my faith. I had little fear, actually I had no fear. As I contemplated these things I realized that much of my faith was built on songs, not just the songs of my childhood, but the songs we sang in the 70's when I first got spirit-filled. These songs were all based on scripture. Let me share parts of some of them for you. Let God arise, let His enemies be scattered, well you know I would say that reflects our situation; another song went "Jehovah-Jireh, my provider, His grace is sufficient for me, God shall supply all my needs, according to His riches in glory, He will give His angels charge over me, for he cares for me. Wow I would say his angels surely protected us in that situation. Another, "I know whom I have believed, and am persuaded that He is able to keep that which I've committed unto Him against that day., Heaven and earth shall pass away, but the Word of the Lord our God shall never pass away; Here's one I like, I will call upon the Lord, who is worthy to be praised, So shall I be saved from my enemies, I will call upon the Lord, and this one, called Victory song, "through our God we shall do valiantly, it is He who will tread down our enemies, we'll sing and shout His victory, Christ is King, the Word has slain the enemy, the earth shall stand and see that through our God we shall do valiantly" and this last one says, The Lord thy God in the midst of thee is mighty, He will save, He will rejoice over thee with joy.

Now I include this because in my early walk, I didn't know the Word of God all that much, and certainly didn't know His promises, but in learning these songs, I learned the promises of the Word, they get to you and help you to grow. We begin to walk the Word, and expect because of His promises that are revealed in song. This is nothing new, as forever in past, songs have encouraged us, supported us, and built us up.

The following is a short reading, but if you look a little closer you will see the whole reading are the titles of songs.

"Love lifted me", I love that song because His love has lifted me from the dark despair of this world into His glorious light. He sat my feet on solid ground, and year after ear He removed the residue that kept me chained to the ways of this world, He gave me understanding, that as he fed me His, manna, I could work my way to become a conductor of His light. He "Washed me with His blood," and made me whiter then snow. His "Old Rugged Cross" made the difference, and with His "Amazing Grace," he said, "Be still My soul." "Holy Holy Holy," Lord God Almighty, how wonderful are your works to me. "What a friend we have in Jesus", as we walk in paths of righteousness. I will continue to, "Stand up, Stand Up for Jesus," as I follow in His footsteps. I am a "Soldier of the Cross," and only ask He "Stand By Me." And though I have walked through the valley of the shadow of death at times, I know that, "Through it All, through it All," I've learned to trust in Jesus, I've learned to trust in Him.

Always I am "Nearer my God to Thee," when I have had a, "Sweet Hour of Prayer," and I am in His "Love that will not Let go." "Jesus is the lover of my Soul," and when I am down and weary, "Precious Lord take my Hand," and, "Lead me Lord," I will, "Trust and Obey."

"Tis so sweet to trust in Jesus," please God, "Open my eyes that I might see," for, "My faith looks up to Thee." I hear the "Voice of one calling, " and "I am Thine, Oh Lord," just "Breath on Me, Breath on me." For we are all "Climbing Jacobs Ladder," that we might be "close to Thee. You call us all to "Seek ye first the Kingdom of God" and as I do, "Every time I hear the Spirit," how grateful I am. I am willing to say, "Lord send me."

:   Oh come all Ye Faithful,' there is a "Spirit in the Night"

"Christ is this worlds Light," let there be a "Silent Night."

"Good Christians friends Rejoice," as we celebrate,

"Jesus the Lover of my soul."

I encourage to learn to sing the songs, it will help your faith grow so when you get into a situation your faith will be able to handle it.

I hope this little book will help you to keep your eyes upon Jesus, look full in his wonderful face, and the things of this world will grow strangely dim in the light of His glory and grace.

If you have found anything helpful in this book, drop me a line. My mail is:

mtkspencer@gmail.com

If you would like to order a book, drop a check for S10.00 and mail it to:

M. Spencer
P.O. 16592
Wilmington, NC, 28408

With your return address.

Made in the USA
Monee, IL
04 August 2021